*bush*
PUBLISHING
& associates

# The Essentials

---

## Discovering How to Develop Your Children's Ministry

### Shawn Scheffler

*The Essentials*
*Discovering How to Develop Your Children's Ministry*
ISBN: 978-0-9836109-6-0
Copyright © 2014 by Shawn Scheffler


Bush Publishing & Associates books may be ordered at www.bushpublishing.com or www.amazon.com.
For further information, please contact:

Bush Publishing & Associates
www.bushpublishing.com / www.k4gministries.com

---

Arise! Dynamite Praise and Worship for Kids!
by Clancy, Brendon And Cathie, p. 85

---

# CONTENTS

# DEDICATION

This book is dedicated to those who have ever
dared to dream and then did it!

# Author's Comments

Dear Reader:

What may only take you a few hours to read has taken me years to learn and then to write. It is my desire that this book will reach across denominational lines and help enlighten the eyes of your understanding concerning children's ministry.

I pray the same joy I have had in writing this book will be the same joy you will have in building the foundation of future generations to come as you develop an effective children's ministry in the local church.

In this book, I pray you will be encouraged to run your race in ministry as a leader or even as a children's minister. I will forever be indebted for the experiences I have gained from teaching children, for the school that taught me how to minister to them, and for the churches and leaders who have allowed me the privilege to have served as their children's pastor and leader.

I want to express my sincere gratitude to everyone who helped make this book possible by offering countless hours of editing, coaching, and encouragement. I want to personally thank Joy Maddox for setting the example in nursery ministry, and for her assistance in providing all the information for our collective efforts in writing the entire nursery section together.

I especially want to say thanks to the generations of children who have received my teachings and whom God has used to give me a purpose in life. May this book help solve problems that might be in your church. May it be the answer to some of the questions you may have been asking! I know you will find this information helpful, and if you need additional assistance or would like to contact our ministry, you can do so at
www.k4gministries.com.

Most importantly, may this information help you to walk worthy of your calling to minister to children!
Let us build the Kingdom of God together.

Rev. Shawn Scheffler

# CHAPTER 1

---

# THE LIFE AND CALLING OF A CHILDREN'S MINISTER AND LEADER

When deciding if you are called to work with children in any ministerial capacity, you must first consider your calling, followed by vision. The first step is to spend time with God and ask Him. If it is only because you possess great knowledge, talents, charisma, or education, then you might be in children's ministry for the wrong reason. What God expects and children need are ministers and leaders whom God has called and qualified.

Though all your attributes are important, offer God your inability to perform anything without HIS help. If you think you are unqualified to hold a baby and teach about the love of God, or lead an entire staff through a week-long Vacation Bible School (VBS), then always remember that God does not call the qualified; He qualifies the called. He prefers us to have an attitude and discipline of depending upon Him, for it is in those times that you will hear from heaven and receive clear direction.

1

Calling is only a small part of an entire race you will success-fully run in the children's ministry. However, without a clear un-derstanding of your calling, there will be several heartaches that could have been avoided.

*Matthew 20:16 says,*
*"Many are called, but few chosen."*

Each child, whether an infant or a sixth grader, will need a minis-ter or leader, and you are that person!

A calling is commissioned by the leading of God. Time spent with Him prior to any ministerial involvement is the very foundation upon which you will build. Do not make a commitment based on a need or simply because you desire to help the church. Needs are always present; however, simple desire will fail you. When you are in the middle of a class or planning a camp and problems mount, YOU MUST KNOW THAT YOUR CALLING IS FROM GOD! A call that does not have a foundation bathed in prayer will leave you unfulfilled and questioning God.

---

### BE A CHOSEN ONE.

---

Children's ministry encompasses such a large area with which you can choose to be involved. God calls nursery leaders, preschool leaders, children's church leaders, and He also calls the children's minister. No matter the calling or the position you hold, it is ex-tremely vital to the life of any church. The position may come with a salary, but what if it doesn't? Your time spent during the class and the preparation for it will not be forgotten by God, or by the children. As you spend time in prayer with God, and before you make any commitments, know what area God is leading you to be involved with. Definitely make sure that it's in an area you enjoy. Remember, it is not always a lifelong commitment. Whatever the time frame may be, God will always reveal it to you.

What if you are already committed to a position and you feel stuck or are not sure if you made the right choice? What if you are positive you are in the right place at the right time? The solution is just as easy as if you are seeking to find out if you should be involved in children's ministry. Take time right now to pray and hear directly from God. Stop reading any further and pray. After you have done this, write in the space provided below what God has revealed to you. Keep what He has shared with you close to your heart.

_____

_____

_____

_____

Now that you have heard from God and your calling is defined by Him, make the decision to serve within your local church based upon that commission. As stated earlier, needs are always present, so ask your pastoral staff, and they will be able to give you direction for each area. My goal is to help you take your calling and turn it into vision, then teach you how to run with that purpose until your race is finished.

*Habakkuk 2:2 says,*
*"Write the vision and make it plain on tablets,*
*that he may run who reads it."*

Vision is ordained by God. Scripture teaches us to write down our vision. The part each member has in that vision is strategic to the overall function of the children's ministry. Keep it simple so you can run with it. A pastor should have a vision written out for the Children's Department. You must find out what God's representative wants for the church. If there is not a written vision, then ask your pastor for one. Be persistent until one is given.

It is so much easier to go somewhere when you have proper directions. Major corporations, mega churches, and even small churches have a vision. They have a Mission Statement that empowers the company, the staff, and all who are influenced by it. **Vision empowers you to succeed for God**. When Jesus called His disciples, He gave them a vision and clear direction.

*Matthew 4:19*
*"Follow Me, and I will make you fishers of men."*

When Jesus sent the disciples out to minister two by two, He empowered them. That vision came from God, and the vision is what the disciples learned to follow.

This is a question I am most often asked: "Are calling and vision really that necessary? After all, I am only babysitting babies in the nursery or teaching crafts to kids." I have even heard statements such as, "Well, I am not the children's minister," or "I only have a small class. What I do can't be so vital that I must personally have a vision from God, can it?" The answer is simple:
ABSOLUTELY!

*Proverbs 29:18 says,*
*"Where there is no vision, the people perish...."*

Take the time right now and write down the vision God has given to your pastor.

_____

_____

_____

_____

The written vision from your pastor is the direction you need to run in this race and achieve it successfully. When athletes prepare for a race, it is understood their goal is to win and run their race according to the rules. It should not be any different with your race. As the children's minister or leader, you are ordained by God to minister to the greatest gift given to a family: their children. God doesn't take your ministerial opportunity lightly and neither should you. He offers great rewards to those who give up much to put the Kingdom of Heaven first.

The service time you miss to serve in the children's ministry, or the time you take off to be a counselor at a camp, directly reflects what you are offering to God as your living sacrifice of service. The vision God has given you comes with great sacrifice. However, when a child you have taught grows up and accomplishes anything, you will see the fruit of your labor. For example, children become husbands or wives, parents, teachers, children's leaders, and many other titles, far too many to mention. YOU HAVE A PART IN THAT! You are chosen by God.

Children are like arrows in the Master's hand.

*Psalm 127:3-5 says,*
*"Behold, children are a heritage from the Lord, the fruit*
*of the womb is a reward. Like arrows in the hand of a*
*warrior, so are the children of one's youth. Happy is*
*the man who has his quiver full of them."*

You (the hand of a warrior) are one of the instruments God uses to point them in the right direction and shoot them off to meet their calling and purpose. When done correctly, they will hit the mark.

Calling and vision are the core elements to the foundation God is building in you and, with time, experience comes and then educational opportunities present themselves. Some advance the ministerial opportunity God has given them by attending specialized schools that train ministers how to teach children. Whatever path God leads you to take, make sure the purpose for which you are running is to win children for Christ. Keep the basics of God's Word as your central core, and follow after His leading in all you do.

The life of the children's ministry leader is very exciting. With our defined calling and vision, there comes a purpose for our lives. The commission which God has personally given to us has guidelines to operate within. It is extremely important for our lives to be an example in all areas.

*Matthew 18:6 says,*
*"Whoever causes one of these little ones who*
*believe in Me to sin, it would be better for him if a*
*millstone were hung around his neck, and he were*
*drowned in the depth of the sea."*

The life you lead as a children's ministry leader will affect the foundations of generations to come. It is a known fact that a house built on a broken foundation cannot stand. Therefore, you must take heed of your lifestyle. In order for a minister/leader to have a successful ministry, you must first have a personal relationship with God.

During the foundation building process of my Christian life and ministry, I had an instructor who took the hand of God and my hand, joining the two together. It was at this time God became my Father. I had been born again for several years, but I didn't know Him as my Father. You will be teaching children about the Father, the Word of God, prayer, and foundational or doctrinal beliefs. Your example begins with your relationship with God and by your time spent in getting to know the Word of God.

Do not substitute the time you spend preparing for a class or an event for a personal walk with God. The children you teach will only grow as far as you develop in your personal walk and knowledge of God. The Bible is the basic foundational tool you will need to help run the race. If you are not reading your Bible, believing it, speaking it, and doing it, then you are deceiving yourself.

*James 1:22 says,*
*"But be doers of the word, and not hearers only,*
*deceiving yourselves."*

For every spiritual event that takes place in the ministry, make sure that you have balanced that experience with the Word of God. Darrell Huffman said, "The Word without the Spirit, you dry up. The Spirit without the Word, you blow up. The Word and the Spirit, you grow up." The Bible balances you. You can't fail when the

Bible is your foundation. I have seen ministers and leaders who have become super spiritual, leaving behind the balance of the Word of God and becoming sidetracked. Due to that, the children suffer, the parents suffer, and the church suffers. You must remain balanced and you can do that as you put God's Word first.

You will find that prayer is an integral part of the children's ministry as well as the leader's life. **As a result of the completed work of Christ, prayer becomes the highway by which you travel to get directly into the Father's presence**. Although knowledge has been gained, education pursued, and then armed with experience, nothing can change a child like prayer. If the heart of a ministry is for the best interest of the children, then it must be bathed in prayer.

I have a dear friend who operated a children's home with his wife. Over the years I have closely noted their journey in ministry and the lives of the children who have been touched by the hand of God through this outreach. The unique difference in what made them successful is the amount of time they spent developing a relationship with their Father in prayer. Any action they took was always covered with a tremendous amount of prayer. The director would often say, "We have bathed this decision in prayer."

---

**As a result of the completed work of Christ, prayer becomes the highway by which you travel to get directly into the Father's presence.**

---

Your involvement in ministry, as the minister or leader, will be conceived in prayer. The ministry opportunities will be birthed through prayer, and your ministry will grow because of prayer.

Put God first in all you do by praying and reading His Word. Can you see that prayer is important? This will require great discipline, but the sacrifice is worth the reward, both in heaven and now.

The life of the children's minister or leader will have a deep foundation in Christian truths. These foundational truths come from the basics of God's Word. My desire is for this book to reach across denominational boundaries and minister to children through their leaders. It is extremely important for you to obtain a Statement of Faith from your church so you know what your guidelines are for teaching and how you will direct those working alongside you.

There is nothing more uncomfortable than teaching outside your boundaries, unless you have been given permission. For example, I have participated in many community-wide outreaches that involved several denominations. Never once have I preached our doctrinal differences, but rather I have centered everything on Jesus, and our need to accept Him as Lord and Savior. You will cover more ground when you do this. Within my church, I preach what we believe with phenomenal results, and you can too as you minister along your denominational beliefs. I encourage you to check your denomination's Statement of Faith for a guideline on what to preach.

As a children's minister/leader, we are called to a life of excellence. It is not something we do, but it is who we are. Everything about us must reflect a life of excellence. I once heard it said, "If it can't be done with excellence, then don't do it at all." Just because other churches are doing a project does not mean you should be doing one. Do not despise the days of small beginnings, and never compare yourself to another person or ministry. There is a mistake that can be the worst in ministry, and it is COMPARISON. The Father has handcrafted you personally, and there are not any two ministries, ministers, or leaders alike.

Your life and excellence go hand in hand. They are inseparable. God will help you in any situation. Excellence must have a foundation in the Word of God, so spend time there and in prayer, and you will develop the foundation for ministerial ethics. Just make sure you hear from God and do exactly what He says when He says, and you will operate in excellence. Be a person of your word, and have a good reputation with those who are around you.

Every year I am held accountable to the following standards in order to maintain my ordination through R.M.A.I. (Rhema Ministerial Alliance International). These guidelines can help you be a better children's minister or leader. As a minister/leader you must set the example in the following areas:

- ☐ In your Christian walk and testimony
- ☐ In marriage and family relationships
- ☐ In fulfilling your responsibilities
- ☐ In your ability to minister
- ☐ In your conduct with the opposite sex
- ☐ In your moral attitudes and conduct
- ☐ In your loyalty to the church/ministry
- ☐ In your commitment and dedication
- ☐ In your submission to authority
- ☐ In your cooperativeness and flexibility
- ☐ In your punctuality

Now that you have some guidelines for conduct in ministry, especially toward children, remember to use them as an example or as a report card for yourself. I challenge you to have those closest to you in the ministry evaluate your performance in the listed guidelines. Use their input as a way to improve your personal ministry and to help hold you accountable to others.

Ralph Waldo Emerson said, "Do not go where the path may lead;

go instead where there is no path and leave a trail." Lead by example and if all you do is get upset because someone told you the truth about your conduct, then you need to realize children really do say it like they see it. In the space provided below write your definition of "excellence," add it to your calling and vision for your life, and watch how God places you in situations where He will get all the glory for the completed work.

In your definition of "excellence," make sure it points to this as a goal: "If it is worth doing, it is worth doing right." According to Webster's Dictionary, the root word of excellence means to excel and it can carry a connotation of being better or greater than another. It may have a flare of superiority, or surpassing someone as in quality and quantity; however, excellence should never have arrogance. Allow your excellence to be a trait found within your position of ministry.

_____

_____

_____

In order to operate in excellence, you must recognize that you have God on your side, and He has accomplished every task with greatness and order. Excellence is something that includes ORGANIZATION, and without organization you will struggle constantly. It is a well thought out, researched, and obedient plan that has been given to you by God. A children's ministry should be the most organized and efficient ministry in the church. This is accomplished through excellence.

Finally, excellence is learned and can be imparted into the lives you will touch. Even if others do not operate with excellence, it is up to you to gain their respect through your diligence. As a children's minister or leader, you will soon find out there is a protocol for ethics in ministry.

*Ephesians 4:11-12 says,*
*"And He Himself gave some to be apostles, some prophets,*
*some evangelists, and some pastors and teachers, for*
*the equipping of the saints for the work of the ministry,*
*for the edifying of the body of Christ."*

As you serve, it is important for you to know your pastor's vision for the Children's Department. In essence, you are doing for the pastor what he would be doing if he could be in all places at all times. With that in mind, it is important for you to gain the respect of your pastor.

There will always be a chain of command in your God-ordained ministry. By following your pastor's vision God has given him, it will be important for you to follow it. My pastor did not give me all the details of what to do, but he has given me the main theme: Kids' World – A modern children's ministry teaching the Word of God. It is my responsibility to now develop a team that runs with **excellence**, has **fun**, works **hard** and **smart**, provides a clean, detail-oriented Department, and **wins souls** for the Kingdom of Heaven. In doing so, I will fulfill what God placed in my pastor's heart for the children's ministry.

When God is in first place each and every day of your life, you can know that all things will work together for your good according to Romans 8:28. I have found that arranging my priorities in the following order has helped me to keep my life and ministry in proper perspective. Strive to put God first. The second most important priority in life is your spouse and family and the extended family members. Thirdly, the ministry calling, and then there is all the work that is required to keep these priorities balanced. As leaders, we must recognize our need to manage these priorities properly. Don't we always have an issue with time? Instead of focusing on the quantity of time, why not let your focus be on the quality of time you can spend within these top priorities?

---

**Vision empowers you to succeed for God.**

---

Finally, it is important for you to follow the leading of God in all you do. Follow the leading of your children's minister or the person set in charge of your Department, and never jump the chain of command. Always speak to the ones above you and trust God to provide your answers through them. Remember, your ministry opportunity is made up of two types of people: Children and Adults. You cannot have one without the other.

Do whatever it takes to reach children in the ministry for they are the fruit of your work. Do whatever it takes to reach adults in the children's ministry, for they become the support group that maintains the foundation of your work. Never underestimate the power of God. Run with excellence. Remember that prayer will change what you have tried to do in all of your own strength, but failed every time because you tried without the help of God. Bathe your position in the children's ministry with the power of God through prayer.

# CHAPTER 2

---

# THE ABC'S OF TEACHING CHILDREN FROM BIRTH THROUGH ELEMENTARY AGE

The following section of this book will help you lay the foundation for the children's ministry within your local church. One really important thing I have learned in life and especially in ministry is that I do not know it all, nor can I do it all. Although I have made myself available to every area of children's ministry, I have enough sense to know that others may be more developed in their calling to children, and I often ask them for their input. The moment you think you know everything, you lose your ability to be taught and risk becoming stagnant in your calling.

This section will include areas of nursery, preschool, and school-aged ministry in the church. One of my dearest friends in the ministry and co-laborer at our church is our nursery director. She has over twenty years of experience in the same place as the nursery/

preschool director, and is always setting the example in ministry. I thank God often for her assistance in providing an example worth writing about. Finally, you will notice much of what is taught concerning learning centers in the next section, can be applied as well in the preschool and school-age ministries.

# NURSERY MINISTRY

Children need a place where they can go and feel safe. Once in an atmosphere of peace, children feel secure and are able to learn. Children need peace and security, and they need to know that their every need is cared for.

Children love to learn about God. In their classrooms they can have an atmosphere where they can praise and worship God as only a child can. When children are placed in an adult setting, they are hindered because adults are in the training mode of teaching respect so the children are told to sit down and be quiet.

We are here to teach the whole child, not just the spiritual side. When a child is old enough to attend school, there will be a solid foundation with no cracks because we teach the child's spirit, soul, and body. We do this through different methods, which begin at a very early age; newborn. Children within the first two years of their life will develop many things including their character and personality. This is a very delicate age and should be treated that way.

From newborn through six months of age, a child learns to roll over, and even scoot across a floor. There will be some small motor skills developing, as in grabbing toys and holding on to them. There also will be a few verbal sounds. From seven months through ten months of age the child learns to crawl, maybe even stand for a while when holding on to things. Between six and eight months, a child learns to sit up on his or her own. Most children from ten to fourteen months learn to walk, and their vocabulary begins to grow quickly. Finally, from fifteen to eighteen months of age, the child will begin to run, fall, and then run some more. Also, some children during this time frame will learn a little bladder control and begin the exciting world of potty training.

Each child will be different, for God is his or her Creator, and He has made each one an individual. He made them to be who they are now and who they will become. Many people write about the different age levels of learning; however, we must view the capabilities that each child may have. It is important to separate children according to their learning abilities so they are free to learn and grow, but in most small churches, having many classes is not realistic. In a small church, it is best to set classrooms as newborn to twenty-four months, two and three year olds, and then four and five year olds. However, some churches place their four and five year olds in with the children's church, which is fine too.

My first statement to you about the ministry to young children would be the most important. **Pray and seek God's advice on those you choose to be your lead teachers.** A child needs to know that the adult in charge wants to be there and wants each child there. The lead teacher must study for the lesson and pray for the children in the class. He or she must have patience with the child, live a godly life at home and in the community, and must be on time. When not on time, it gives the child the idea that you do not want to be there. The lead teacher must be knowledgeable in the Word of God, hold the vision for the Nursery Department, and not be a taskmaster.

Every child's minister or leader will need time in the adult services to receive from God weekly. This is very important. You cannot expect someone to minister to the children if he or she has given out and given out until there is nothing left to give. The leader needs the corporate anointing, so please make sure your ministers and leaders are in at least one adult service each week and two if possible. God knows their needs and will meet them as they serve Him. God not only ministers to the adults, but to the children as well.

If we as teachers are agitated or distracted, we find it difficult to receive from God. So when children arrive, they should have a few minutes of the minister's undivided attention. Allow the helpers to take care of the children who arrive earlier. Be sure to make eye contact with children and talk to them. Let children know how special they are and that you are happy to see them. Then turn to the parents and do the same for them. The parents will gain an assurance that their child is wanted and will be well taken care of.

Be sure to give each child your special attention at least once during each center in some way or another. You want children to know that God made him or her, and that God loves them. Finally, God has a plan for their life. There will be times for some children when there is a spirit of fear in separating from their parents. You need to be prayed up and exhibit lots of patience to minister to the child and the parent, because it can be difficult for these children. The most important thing is not to allow the child to manipulate Mom, Dad, or the Grandparent. If you are able, assure the person leaving the child that the child will be fine.

If the child does not settle down within five to ten minutes after the parent has left the room, then contact the parent to come back and love on the child. The parent should not remain in the room for more than ten minutes and should never be left alone with other children unattended. If a parent does not want to leave the child, then they must return to the adult services with the child. This is for the other children's safety as well as yours and for the well-being of the entire church.

Children need their own place to praise and worship God. When a newborn to five years of age is kept in the sanctuary, they can possibly become a distraction for the parents, the congregation, and the pastor. The children will become bored and insist on attention, and the child will not learn as much as they would in their own setting.

A learning center is a good tool to use in teaching a basic truth to a child and reinforcing that truth. The basic truth is found in the memory verse. The lesson is what teaches the basic truth and the centers help reinforce the truth presented in each lesson. Centers also help to keep children's attention, which will help them keep out of trouble. The centers should be set up for nursery age children with a maximum time of ten to fifteen minutes. Changing direction and moving on to a new center will keep the children interested in what they are learning. **Now is a good time to remember that the children will be as excited about what they are doing as you are, so show your excitement as well.**

There are several ways you can set up centers. Please be sure to individualize them to your specific church needs. Here is a list of centers that can be used:

**Play Acting:** A time to dress up and pretend to be someone else. Maybe they want to be a Mommy or a Daddy. Be sure to play with them and talk to the children.

**Praise and Worship:** Teach them how to praise and worship God. This is so important for their foundation. When we praise and worship God and draw near to Him, He draws near to us. Our problems will become very small and solutions will come to light. Know the songs you plan to have in praise and worship. Be sure to have praise music and worship music. Talk to the children about worship and what it means to God.

Children love to dance, jump, shout, make motions, and be loud, so help them to do this. When they see you in adult services, be sure they are seeing you just as excited as you are in class! This is very important because children are very perceptive and know when you are being truthful with them.

> **Now is a good time to remember that the children will be as excited about what they are doing as you are, so show your excitement as well.**

Praise and Worship is a good time to ask everyone if they need to pray about anything. Praise and Worship is a form of prayer and a time to let them know that God hears both our prayers and our praise. We try to have music that will line up with the teaching for the day, but the most important part of Praise and Worship is to teach the children about worshipping God and how happy it makes Him.

**Memory Verse:** The memory verse is the key to the lessons. It is important for all the children to learn verses in the Bible. Do not believe that if the children are young, they are unable to learn the verses. When children can sit in front of a television and repeat every scene in their favorite movie, they can memorize a Bible verse. The idea is to make it exciting. You can put music or rhythm to the verse, or maybe play a game to help them memorize it. Giving out prizes for those who have the verse memorized is another incentive way of teaching.

**Arts and Crafts:** If you bring a craft into the classroom, make sure it is suitable for the age you are teaching. If the children are too young to know how to cut, have your craft precut so they can concentrate on coloring and gluing. Toddlers from fifteen months to two years old may want you to teach how to hold a crayon and how to use it. This will take one-on-one supervision because most children this age will want to eat the crayons. Once again, it is important in this center to teach the basic truth of the lesson that is taught for the day, so be sure the artwork or craft points back to the basic truth.

**Small Motor Skills:** This is a time to have puzzles, blocks, or some kind of cutting project ready for the children. You could even have all three going on at the same time. Just make sure you have someone at each center. If you only have two workers, then only have two items going on in this center. Be prayed up and prepared for the children to help them apply their memory verse in the center. For example, creation: With building blocks, you could talk about how God built all of us. Or in the case of Noah's ark – With building blocks, you could talk about how God gave Noah the wisdom on how to build the Ark.

**Large Motor Skills:** If the weather is nice outside, this would be a great time to take the children out to play. Try to have a fenced in play area, and make sure it isn't muddy outside because they will have church clothes on. Otherwise, riding toys, inside slides, bouncing balls, and games with skipping or jumping can be used. There are many tools that can be utilized to teach the children large motor skills.

**Quiet Center:** During the quiet center, you can read books or watch a video that relates to the main lesson and the basic truth of the lesson. There is a lot of material available on the Internet. Always view material and books brought in to make sure they line up to the Word of God. Some books have magic and wizardry in them, so steer clear of these books.

**Free Time:** This is a time when the children can check out the rest of the toys available for play. If you have a large class, this center may not be advisable. Sometimes this center can be used in between the other centers, especially if the children have been sitting for a while. Allow children some time to run around so they can expend their energy. This will help them focus better when you call them back together.

**Lesson:** This center is very important. Be sure to know your material and get excited about what the children are learning for the day. Yes, I said that correctly: "Get excited about what they are learning for the day." When you teach the children, expect to learn, too. Have some way of getting the children to be involved in the lesson. For example, if you are teaching about Noah's Ark, have some of the children snap fingers, while others clap, and others make the wave sound. This way it makes a sound like it is raining and thundering.

When it comes to the lessons, you will need to pray and seek God's direction. Our church has designed a set of twelve lessons that we use in our Nursery Department. You will need to find what works for your church and your church's budget. It is important to teach the whole child. This is why we focus on large and small motor skills as well as the Word of God. For example, if you want to build a foundation but forget to add the rock that goes in the cement mixture, you would not have a solid foundation. We teach the whole child: spirit, soul, and body so that each child receives a solid foundation.

**Rewards and Prizes:** Schedule a time close to the end of class to give out rewards for bringing a Bible to class, a friend, or an offering. You can also give out rewards for participating in the class activities. WOW! They love it when they get a prize. You will want to keep the prize simple. I have found that for this age, too many choices are not a good thing, so I have small candies, rings, and stickers. The children enjoy the rewards, and it gives them something to work towards. It also prompts good behavior.

Now it is time to discuss setup and teardown for the class. It is important for leaders to arrive in their classroom at least thirty minutes prior to service so they will have time to pray and set their classroom up to receive the children. Most children will begin to arrive anywhere from fifteen to twenty minutes early. All workers are to remain in the classroom until all teardown has been completed. This includes workers. It is important to train your lead teachers to keep everyone until the last job is completed. You can do this by providing workers with a sheet that outlines what is expected from them for each service.

Now to address the administration functions of the Nursery Department's Director. You will have plenty to do each service so it is very important that you get a team of workers so you do not find yourself doing all the work. There will always be a need for getting more people involved with the nursery ministry. A few suggestions that I have found helpful include:

- Invite your pastor to teach on the benefit of helping in the church.
- Show live or recorded videos of the classroom on monitors throughout the church.

☐      Effectively advertise your Department inside
the church using pictures of the children
while in nursery.

☐      Hold a special meeting and teach
about your Department.

It is very important to screen each applicant. Do not become so desperate for workers that you allow someone in the classroom who may cause harm to a child. Not everyone is meant to serve in this area, so establish a set of qualifications for the workers. I have discussed ways you can use to obtain workers, but once you have them, it is also critical to keep them. Be sure to get to know your team, praise them for having a heart to minister to the children, and thank them for their time. It takes a lot to get to church early and then to have to leave late. When you praise your workers, be sure the praise is sincere. Just like children, workers can tell when you are saying something just to be saying it.

It is important for the workers to attend at least one adult service a week as I stated earlier and more if possible. They will be unable to minister if they are dry and without the Word of God. All of us must continually be filled with the Word of God on a regular basis in order to keep our faith established. I have found that I always need to be available in case a worker needs my help. If you check on a class and find it is out of control, do not leave. Help the leader to gain control, and remind the worker that he or she can call on you if they need your help.

Listen to your workers. Let them know you care. If possible, schedule the workers where they are best suited and keep the same schedule from one month to the next. If you need to adjust the schedule, be sure to contact your team so they can check to see the new schedule. When doing this, make sure you have extra copies to give out as reminders.

Finally, I will address the need for forms and their importance. Yes, the paper trail. Forms will help protect the church, leaders, workers, and children. We have an enemy who likes to wreak havoc on the church; however, with proper paperwork, usually you will have enough information to protect yourself and the church. There have been times when my pastor has asked about a certain date, who was in the classroom, and if there is any information regarding incidents that happened during the class. In today's world, it is very important to have an overflow of paperwork.

In our church, we have several forms that we use in all departments to keep us organized. They include: The Class Report, Absentee Form, Supply Request Form, Maintenance Request Form, and the Child Information Sheet. Design your forms to meet the needs of your church. By having a well-equipped team of workers, the right curriculum, and the tools you need to minister to infants, you will have a very successful nursery ministry.

# PRESCHOOL MINISTRY

In the fall of 1991, I had my first experience with preschoolers. The classroom only included three year olds, but on average there were anywhere from thirty to forty children in the class. Considering that the church I had attended as a young man only had twenty people in an evening service, I was overwhelmed. My opinion was that three year olds were extremely safe and friendly. However, I soon found out preschoolers have unique needs because of characteristics they exhibit.

The life of a preschooler and your ministry to them is vital to the church. God carefully watches what you do with preschoolers. Children are to be seen and they are to be heard.

*In Matthew 19:13-15 we read the story of how Jesus and His disciples responded to children:*

*"Then little children were brought to Him that He might put His hands on them and pray, but the disciples rebuked them. But Jesus said, 'Let the little children come to Me, and do not forbid them; for of such is the kingdom of heaven.' And He laid His hands on them and departed from there."*

A child will have the greatest opportunity to receive Christ at this age if you are dedicated to teaching them the truths of God's Word. Evangelism to this age group is a must. Your message must be that of love, acceptance, comfort, peace, security, and sincerity. Children know if they are welcomed in your church.

When teaching preschoolers, you must remember that they need their own space. Smaller churches often have to be mobile and are limited in what space they can offer to the Children's Department. You as the children's minister or leader will have to learn to be flexible. One church I know meets in a school and has to set up for every service, then tear down after every service. The church allocated the cafeteria to the preschool and school-aged classes. The children's director purchased popup canvas tents and has two 10x20 sections. One section is for junior kids' church (preschoolers) and the other is for kids' church. This director found artists in the church to paint backdrops that coordinated with the curriculum themes. **Never allow your small beginnings to hinder the work of God in your heart.**

All preschoolers have a desire to belong. You have the opportunity to provide this and fulfill their desire. The personality of each child will determine how the class will function. There will be energetically outgoing children, quiet and peaceful, compliant, shy, well-educated, and even special needs children. Your plan must meet their needs. When planning your class, it is important for you to be consistent. The curriculum, the leaders, and the classroom will all provide a safe and secure environment for the preschooler.

Every great preschool class must be properly staffed. A parent will be able to receive during the adult service if they know their children are taken care of and safe. Usually a church will have a service on Sunday morning, Sunday evening, and Wednesday evening. The goal is to have a class for each of these services and during special services. Do not have a class just to have one. Determine with your pastor which services to begin. Then as it develops, add another service. Children deserve the best, and you can give it to them.

> **Never allow your small beginnings to hinder the work of God in your heart.**

Pray that God will direct you to the leaders you have need of, that He will show you who they are just as He did when Jesus called the disciples. Follow Jesus' example in recruiting for the ministry, and remember that God called Him too. Jesus knew He had a calling, vision, and divine purpose. He knew it couldn't be done without leaders. So as the Spirit of God directed Him, He found them, called them, and then led them into greater works. Jesus would simply say, "Come, follow Me." He prayed and God revealed to Him those who were to be His leaders. Since God did that for Jesus, then know He will do that for you! Ultimately, children's ministry belongs to the Lord, not you.

When developing your class, remember not to despise your small beginnings. When determining the classroom needs, visit day cares for color ideas, toys, games, and equipment. Day cares have state guidelines and laws they have to adhere to, and a church should be just as considerate of, if not more compliant, to these standards. Now, what if your department only has three or maybe five children, your church budget is zero, but your desire costs a fortune? It is really simple. Take an inventory of what your church has. You can even inquire among the church members about what they may have around their homes. So much of what you are looking for the church members may already have and are willing to give it away. Let them know! Always take your needs to God and believe for Him to provide them.

*Hebrews 11:6 says,*
*"But without faith it is impossible to please Him [God]...."*

He always rewards those who are seeking after Him. John 15:7 and 11 teaches that you can abide in Him, ask what you desire, and this is all so our joy might be complete.

I will never forget the time I needed a puppet stage for our Department, and God provided it through a church member. It was more than I could have ever dreamed. I still have that puppet stage, and my joy still remains full as a result of God's provision. These preschoolers belong to God. It is His desire for them to have what they need.

Whenever I have a need, I prepare a list of items that are in excellent shape (this avoids junk items and makes givers think about their gift), and then I put it before the church. After **following up** with church members, our needs are often met above and beyond. My pastor, Reverend Jerry Piker, once said, "If it is worth doing, then it is something that must be done with excellence; and if it can't be, then don't do it until it can be." People won't know there is a need unless you ask them. A church should not have a preschool class unless it can be done with excellence and **you are the one to do it**. Now that you have a place, the items you need to use, and the leaders, what should you teach? When selecting a curriculum, here are a few questions to ask:

☐ Does it follow our Tenets of Faith?
☐ Can it be reused? (This saves a lot of money.)
☐ Is it teacher friendly or do you have to have a doctorate to understand it?
☐ Is it learning-center friendly?

As you use these questions as a guideline, you can determine what your church needs will be. Always bathe your decisions in prayer, and get the leading of God in the process. Write out your answers to these questions and present them to your pastor for a final decision. You will find a greater success rate in teaching the right curriculum if you have done your homework before you present it to your pastor.

In the nursery section, you heard about learning centers; and in a preschool class you must have them implemented. The impact of using centers within the Preschool Department will allow diversity in the spiritual training of the children. Preschoolers learn while they play, so you will have an opportunity to teach in every aspect during the time they spend in the class. Do not underestimate the value a learning center can have, even in a small church.

I always take the average service time in our church and then divide it by 10 to 15 minutes. For example, a typical service for preschoolers can be over two hours: 120/15=8. Your class should have eight different learning activities. Once it has been determined how many centers are needed to cover a service, always, always, always overplan. Have a few activities planned that can be pulled out if needed.

In conclusion, remember as a children's minister or leader, you must have a vision that gives purpose to what you do. Make sure to write the vision out, and run with it as you reach preschoolers for Christ. This is such an amazing age to be able to minister to, so give them your best.

# ESTABLISHING A CHILDREN'S CHURCH

This book could never contain all of the information needed to teach and train this age level. I have learned that all children change on a daily basis. What a kindergartner expects out of children's church will be entirely different from what a fifth grader expects. Yet, in many churches, all of these grades/ages will be combined into one class. Therefore, the challenge is to be able to include these expectations into one service.

Many would think it all begins with the curriculum, maybe the classroom, or even all the fancy bells and whistles to capture a child's attention. Although atmosphere is important in keeping a child interested, the first and foremost tool to develop would be the children's minister and then the leadership. This leadership in a small church might only be two people and at best three. Just make the commitment within your heart to serve your pastor's vision, and expect your area to develop into many leaders.

*Galatians 6:9 says,*
*"And let us not grow weary while doing good, for in due*
*season we shall reap if we do not lose heart."*

Your church can effectively reach school-aged children. Therefore, you must have a vision that will create a purpose and a plan for this Department. Make sure to write down where you are going. It should have, as the foundation, the pastor's Vision Statement he has given to you. Write out that vision here:

_____

_____

_____

_____

As a children's minster/leader, it is important for you to know your vision and not get discouraged along the way. No matter the size of the Department, give it your entire focus during each service. In the first church where I was a children's minister, there were plenty of classrooms, a large resource room, and a fellowship hall that doubled as a children's church. However, there were only a few kids. Their ages ranged from preschool to fifth grade. We never gave anything less than our very best, and as a result, our leadership and the number of children we ministered to grew over a period of time.

**The church today has the greatest opportunity to capture the attention of a child by developing a ministry that involves both the natural and the supernatural.** One without the other leaves the class empty and everyone involved without God's best. If all you do is take care of the natural items in the class and you deny the power of God, you will be left with an emptiness that can only be filled by God's supernatural presence. On the other hand, if all you do is offer the supernatural, it will fall apart without the natural planning and organization. The two must work hand in hand, and you are the one to accomplish this.

The children you minister to today are not the same generation of children from five or even ten years ago. This will hold true until Jesus comes again. **It is our responsibility to reach the children of our time within their time.** Although our message stays the same, our methods must always be fresh, creative, age-appropriate, and modern. There will never be a time that you have to sacrifice the basic truths of the Word of God to accommodate a modern children's ministry. If you do, then you are missing the point of **reaching the children of our time in their time.**

> **The church today has the greatest opportunity to capture the attention of a child by developing a ministry that involves both the natural and the supernatural.**

If you refuse to refresh in changing times, then it will cost you in your ability to continue to minister to school-aged children. I learned this the hard way and at a great cost to the growth of a children's camp I oversaw for several years. I learned that my methods of ministry needed to be current with those to whom I was ministering. In this situation, my administration tools were outdated and lacked the impact that other camps were offering via the Internet, and social media. Another example took place at a children's lock-in I had planned. I learned that the music I found so near and dear to my heart for the last fifteen years was not even close to what the children listened to during their own free time. These life lessons are so important when you are a children's minister or leader. Take this into consideration when developing the overall plan for your children's church.

Two excellent tools to incorporate into the development of children's church are learning centers and large group settings. Learning centers have already been discussed in the nursery section of this book. However, a large group setting is basically taking the same format and just adding more children. Instead of the children moving from center to center, the class participates in a service where the children's minister and leaders move from one action of the service to the next. A large group can consist of ten to more than a hundred children.

I have used both formats with few and many children. The challenge with large groups is to keep their attention and for them to focus on what is being taught. The best way to do this is with audience participation. I have found that separating the boys from the girls automatically causes participation and competition. When you are calling upon either group, they want their side to win. Use this to your advantage when teaching the Bible verse, playing a game, or even in worship. In the large group setting, the goal is to focus them on Christ and use methods that create in them the desire to want more of Him. Use what God has placed in you to teach your class.

Later on in this section, you will find ways to prepare a lesson plan that will include learning centers and large group settings dependent upon the size of the class. Take ideas from this section and develop numerous activities that will need to be accomplished during the service. This is also a great avenue to train your leaders. By giving leaders a portion of the overall service, their confidence and trust in the Holy Spirit's leading will increase, and your ability to delegate will continue to flourish.

When determining what your church will begin to do for children, it is important to evaluate certain components; for example, the availability for a classroom. Some children's churches are fellowship halls, a small room, a cafeteria, hallway, closet, or even a combined children's and youth room. Think about what you currently have available, and then determine what can be done for the room to make it inviting for children. Next, you must plan out the length of your service. Will it be from the moment church members start arriving? Will it start after adult praise and worship? Will you have the parents check their children in before service and then check out after service? You must know the needed time in order to fulfill the vision of the pastor.

It would be very easy to say your church can offer a children's service, but if you do not have enough leaders, you can easily end up frustrated. You must avoid frustration at all costs. **Leaders are the key to a successful classroom.** They truly are the most valuable resource a church will ever have.

In Ephesians 4:11 it is clear that God has called many to different functions in the Body of Christ and not all of us will be preachers. However, we are all called to help assist in the church. God doesn't call the qualified; He qualifies the called.

Now that you have leaders in place, it is always wise to have two leaders at every service and in each classroom because it provides accountability. Check with any local day care to get an idea of their student-to-teacher ratio. As the church, there should at minimum be the same standard if not better. Many churches find it difficult to recruit leaders, and the reason for that is because they are not following the example Jesus gave. He knew what His vision was for His ministry. He knew how many disciples it would take to fulfill the plan. He personally called His disciples.

---

**Leaders are the key to a successful classroom.**

---

The church, on the other hand, may place guilt trips on parents and church members to teach in the classrooms. There are repetitive pleas in the bulletin; tired, grumpy workers; and far too many sob stories to count. This does not build respect, and it certainly will not build a kids' church that will have children begging their parents to take them to church. Change your recruiting methods, call leaders, then train and teach them continuously. Make the children's ministry a joy and it will grow.

Now that there has been a space laid out for a classroom and leaders are in place, the next question would be, "What do you teach?" If your church is considering a children's program, contact other churches in your area or even in your denomination to see if they have any curriculum they are not using that could be purchased or borrowed. I know far too many churches that have years worth of curriculum that is collecting dust in a dark, dingy closet down in the basement where no one knows it even exists. Ask them for it and plan out your class.

When deciding on a curriculum, make sure learning centers, praise, worship, and games can be inserted. If they are already available, then be flexible and add what is important to be taught to the children. Do not think for one moment that a lesson is set in stone, and you have to finish the whole thing in one class setting. I have found within just a few short years of experience in dealing with curriculum that there is almost always too much material to cover and retain for a child. If the children can't even remember what you have taught because there were too many points covered, then you have a problem and need to reconsider how much you are willing to teach in a given time frame.

What you teach must be centered on the foundational doctrines of your denominational beliefs. Your church should have Tenets of Faith or a Doctrinal Beliefs Statement. Do not merely avoid certain curriculum choices because it does not fit into the box of your denominational beliefs. I have learned to use Assembly of God, Southern Baptist, Charismatic, and Methodist curriculum. I have written my own curriculum for years as well as other materials. Your church may have you add some teachings to balance or reinforce your doctrinal beliefs. Just make sure your pastor is in agreement and you have his/her approval. Overall, I have never seen a child suffer because I taught from the Bible. Keep it simple and you'll never run out of lessons to teach.

My next goal is to share with you some ideas about effectively planning out your class with lesson plans. It is important for you to have them written out on a piece of paper or on your electronic device so that whoever reads it may easily follow along.

*Habakkuk 2:2 says,*
*"Write the vision and make it plain on tablets,*
*that he may run who reads it."*

Who would have guessed that Habakkuk would have known about modern-day electronic devices called tablets?
Without a written plan, you will plan to fail. Without a plan, what

direction will you or a team have to follow? While doing an Easter play, I failed to write out what was in my heart and what I saw, so when I had to lead children and leaders, there was no sense of direction. Can you imagine what happened?

What is a lesson? Webster's Dictionary defines it as something to be learned, a course of instructions, a rebuke or reproof, an exercise that needs to be learned for one's safety.

What is a plan? Webster's Dictionary defines it as a scheme for making, doing, or arranging something such as a project or schedule. **A lesson plan is a set of instructions used in making a project that helps others learn something for their own benefit.** There are many lesson plan styles from which to choose. Remember to select one that best fits your style. Many curriculums include a lesson plan for you to follow. I have found that the following guideline has helped me to write effective lesson plans for years.

In order to make effective lesson plans, understand the importance of the goal, unit theme, scriptures for the lesson, memory verse, date, and the outline of the service. When I come up with a goal, I state in a simple sentence what I want the children to walk away with from the service. An example could be: "Each student will understand the value of walking in the God-kind of love." Next, I have found it to be beneficial to teach in unit themes that focus on an area for about three months or longer if it is a universal theme. For example, the gifts of the Holy Spirit would be a universal theme, but each of the attributes would be an individual theme.

It is important to list the scriptures you study to teach the lessons, especially when you need to refer to them while teaching. The memory verse is the scripture you want a child to learn and know. Make sure the verse is age appropriate and is not five sentences long. It is not wrong for you to adjust the verse, making it easier for children to memorize. With so many translations of the Bible available, you can't go wrong with finding one they understand. For example, if you use the King James, make sure to place the word "you" into a section that may say "thee." Children don't talk with thee's and thou's; they speak in you's and how's.

There are many reasons to date your lesson plan. For example, it might be helpful in establishing your own curriculum someday, for parent involvement, recording purposes, and even as a reminder to let you know when the last time this lesson was taught. Finally, the outline of your service will be a plan you have made to meet the demands of a two- or three-hour ministry time. Never underestimate your planning, and feel free to add more items than what you think you may need to do. Here is an example of what I have used. Note that each category can be deleted or added to, depending on what is planned for the service. The more consistent I have been in using the same format, the easier it has been for our team to follow. Take a look and see if it's a style that might just fit as a lesson plan for you to use.

# LESSON PLAN

Goal:

Unit Theme:

Scriptures:

Memory Verse:

Date:

Service Outline: (Any one of the 15 below or what you may add)

1.      Welcome
2.      Announcements
3.      Offering
4.      Praise Song
5.      Memory Verse
6.      Praise Song
7.      Worship Songs
8.      Lesson
9.      Memory Verse Review Game
10.     Games
11.      Snacks
12.      Learning Centers
13.      Group Time
14.      Review Games
15.      General Store (Reward Center)

In this section, I have covered how to set up the classroom, select a leader, choose curriculum, and design lesson plans. Now it is vital for the finishing touches to be added to your newly developed kids' church. You must have some basic skills in how to decorate your room in such a way that children will want to come back each week. Visual aids are significant in the overall impact they will have upon your classroom. Basically, they include anything you can get your hands on to help get the main teaching theme across to the children. A visual aid can be as extravagant and expensive as you like, or it can be as simple as what your budget can afford. A former teacher of mine at Rhema Bible Training College, Judy Collins, once said, "Your mind is like a parachute; if you don't unlock it, it won't work." Remember this little formula when planning your visual effects for the classroom. We retain 10 percent of what we hear, 20 percent of what we read, 50 percent of what we hear and read, 90 percent of what we do, and 95 percent of what is set to music. Effective visual aids will need considerable planning. Do not present anything that has not been given prior consideration or planning. We never know who is observing our props. Finally, make sure the visual aids produce a child-friendly environment.

Children are not adults and their settings should not be the same as you would find in an adult sanctuary. Your classroom visuals are being compared by children to places such as restaurants, entertainment parks, television shows, and movies. Awesome classroom decorations do not have to cost a fortune. Do one project at a time and even include the children in the planning of the room theme. I have found it easier to plan the classroom with a general theme, and then I accommodate the season of the year into that theme. For example, you may have a castle theme (King's Kids), an old Spanish country, a shopping mall, space age, musical place, or even a Big Top Circus theme.

I am a strong supporter of excellence in what is done in ministry. This holds true for decorations and visual aids. Excellence in this area takes time, money, talent, vision, purpose, planning, and then work. Small churches can do big things if they will trust God for their needs. The first church where I became a children's minister was an example of not despising the days of small beginnings. Our Department was redecorated in a short period of time, but these were some of the steps I took, and still use to this day no matter where I serve.

I take one step at a time. God orders our steps, not our leaps and bounds. Start with what you have. Ask members in your church for their help. Ask your pastor if you can use the monies coming in that are marked for the Children's Department for a special project. Have your leaders and the children believe God for what you will need. Begin the process of revamping the classroom. Make everything as portable as possible so it can be used for other purposes, such as Vacation Bible School, Conferences, and camps, if needed. Your equipment and visual aids are helpful in maintaining the learning environment and keeping the children engaged. Give it your best and keep the classroom current or up to date.

Never believe a small church can't do something for children on a grand scale. Presently, I attend a church with an average attendance of around 100 people. We have over 24,000 square feet for our Children's and Youth Department. Our combined children's churches are larger than the adult sanctuary. You might ask why, and my answer is that my pastor and the church have a heart to reach children and youth. Even when there was only a small space for the children in the early days of the church, the pastor and church still had a heart for children. To have the best, it costs money and takes time. In today's world, if our small churches want to reach children, then your pastor and church must have the heart for it, and your classrooms need to reflect that heart. Will you believe God?

The final area that we need to discuss in developing the children's church is the use of games. Children love to have fun. The service must have a healthy balance of games in order to maintain the attention of the diverse age levels you will be teaching. With modern technology, game ideas are endless. Your classroom should be full of many fun and exciting times. Your public library is also an excellent resource for new game ideas. When planning games, the number of children and the age levels will determine if that game is appropriate to be played. Always think beyond the borders of ideas and believe for witty inventions and ways to adapt them to your service. Never underestimate the ability or desire of a child to compete during games. I have seen preschoolers outmaneuver elementary students in order to win. Oftentimes, in smaller settings, I will have to divide the group into two teams. Usually it is boys against girls, or I will line them up and count them off. Make sure that whatever is decided, each team needs to be as equal as possible. Now go have some fun and play some games.

In conclusion, when developing your children's church you will need a lot of equipment to minister to children: visual aids, chairs, chalkboards, dry eraser boards, smart boards, projectors, televisions, DVDs and players, music systems, crayons, glues, markers, scissors, and the list is endless. It will not be built overnight, but start asking your church members. Make a wish list, pray over it, present it, and expect BIG things to happen and you will see BIG results. As the children's minster or leader of a small church, it is easy to feel pressured into buying everything yourself. If your resources allow you to do so, great! However, don't max out your personal budget to override God's ability to provide through His people. I learned the hard way that what I was trying to provide on my own and with my own financial resources, God had already made a way for it, but He couldn't get it to me because I did not ask Him for it.

# CHAPTER 3

---

# ADMINISTRATION AND BUDGET

**I am convinced the reason God created trees was to make sure I could have a paper trail for everything I do.** In this section there will be an extensive amount of information that will help you in the governing of a Children's Department. Your pastor and church may already have a set format, and if they do, make sure you ask them for it and adhere to that format. No matter the size of your church, do what needs to be done with excellence. Paperwork is my least favorite thing to do in children's ministry, yet it is one of the most vital things I can do to communicate with my pastor, parents, and the church.

> **If it wasn't for the assistance of my team in their helping with the day-to-day operations of the ministry, I could not be where I am today.**

Effective administration of the Children's Department will include lots of paperwork. What you put on paper sets the vision of God into place. It is important for you to write down goals on a regular basis. The average children's minister and leaders stay in a church for less than two years. One of the reasons for this might be that no one has ever taught them to have a written plan or goal(s). **If it wasn't for the assistance of my team in their helping with the day-to-day operations of the ministry, I could not be where I am today.** Surround yourself with people who will help you. I repeat to you the need for Keeping It Simple Sweetie (K.I.S.S.). Your leaders already have enough to do, so make sure their service paperwork is simple, self-explanatory, and sufficient for reports.

In regards to reports, the best one is the one you could obtain about your leaders. A pastor who values professionalism and is a protector of the children will run state background checks on all of his/her children and youth workers. These can be obtained easily from your state, and though the cost might be expensive, the benefits of having cleared members of your team will speak volumes to the security you offer to parents, the church, and your community.

> **The more prepared you are, the more organized you will be and the more you will have to give to others in ministry.**

Have you ever asked yourself the question, "Whatever will I do with all this paperwork, reports, and information that I obtain while working in the children's ministry?" Just remember that everything, and I mean everything, has a place in effective organization. It may be all over the counter, shoved in a box, neatly filed away in cabinets, and even stored on your computer, but it needs to be organized. **The more prepared you are, the more organized you will be and the more you will have to give to others in ministry.** Organizing how your administration functions will be labor intensive up front, but it will **make** and **save** you time in your years of ministry to children. Like gasoline is to a car, organization is the fuel that helps to keep your ministry running in an excellent manner.

Creating an ever-growing filing system will lay the foundational support for the work you will do with children. This system will allow you to place those "Ah ha!" notes you took, or that idea you had or heard, and even the article you read that would change the course of your classroom. Whatever will you do with all those lesson plans you have written out or even the VBS material you just had to have? Not to mention those reports and request forms you have to fill out in order to have a fund-raiser or even a children's event. By having a system that allows you to file this information, you will be able to pull out what you need when you need it and not have to say, "Now where did I put that?"

I have a leader who took this filing system to heart, and every time I ask her to teach a class, she reminds me that she is prepared because of the information I shared with her and will share with you. Your filing system will help you fulfill what God has called you to do and it can make others see that you are taking your work seriously. **The easiest thing to do is not to do anything.** The hardest thing to do is to be disciplined enough to care about what you are doing and do it so others can follow your example. Just think about how others will be blessed because you cared enough to be organized.

> **The easiest thing to do is not to do anything.**

While organizing the administrative section of your children's ministry, remember to K.I.S.S. (Keep It Simple Sweetie)! I have found that the easier I keep it, the more organized I am. Are you committed to serving in your church and going beyond the average two-year time frame that a leader is in a church? Then you will soon find out that your filing system will change over time and help keep you better organized. What you once thought was important may change. You might even go all computer-based for your filing needs.

Here are a few categories that I have adapted from personal notes from college and that I have added over the years. I believe it will help you be better organized.

First, you must start out with a filing cabinet or even a cardboard box, and yes, even your computer. Of course, it all depends on what you have or can get your hands on. Within this filing system, include the following five sections:

1. Children's Ministry Business
2. Getting Organized
3. Daily Communications
4. Resources
5. Curriculum

Now let's take each section and add to it what will be helpful in maintaining an ever growing filing system.

**Children's Ministry Business** could have the following topics in its section:

1. Notes from workshops, classes, or seminars
2. Children's characteristics and developmental needs
3. Health and Safety
4. Leadership-training material (Volunteer Training)
5. Children's teaching ideas

6. Lesson Plans (Plans that you have created)

7. Reproducible items

(Items you have legal permission to reproduce)

**Getting Organized** could have the following topics in its section:

1. Teachers' manuals (Samples and ideas for manuals)
2. Forms (Samples and design ideas from others)
3. Scheduling ideas
4. Event planning
5. Volunteers

(Leaders, applications, and notes regarding leaders)

6. Completed Activities

(Make sure to include notes of things you did that worked well or did not work well, purchase requests, cost of events, and feedback. All this will help in future planning.)

7. Vacation Bible School, camps, crusades

(Include ideas for curriculum, cost of events, event materials, and past, present, and future items needed.)

**Daily Communications** could have the following topics in its section:

1. Purchase Requests
2. Current and previous schedules
3. Ministry Correspondence

(Include pertinent e-mails, copies of letters sent and received.)

4. Classroom and department records
5. Current catalogs
6. Hard to find Supplies

(Items that you don't use every day, but need once in a while.)

7. Investigate (Ideas you want to know more about.)

8. Birthdays (Children and Leaders)
9. Special Events (Such as parties, mission projects, etc.)

**Resources** could have the following topics in its section and should be age- appropriate by the Department. For example: Nursery, Preschool, or Elementary.

1. Current Inventory On Hand
2. Skits (Puppets, Drama Team, or even video production links.)
3. Puppets (What you want, patterns, etc.)
4. Costumes (What you want, patterns, etc.)
5. Music
6. Games
(Categorized in how they can be used; i.e., indoor/outdoor)
7. Bulletin Board ideas
8. Season information
9. Craft ideas
10. Learning centers
11. Etc.
(The section you place those documents you don't know where to file.)

**Curriculum** will be ever-expanding, will soon outgrow your filing system, and will end up being the largest space-taking section in your office or resource room. In your main filing system, you will eventually have just the scope and sequence of the material you have on hand. Every curriculum you purchase will have an order to how it should be taught according to the writer. Make sure you file it in such an order. Depending upon the type of curriculum you buy, it may come in a binder or special packaging. Maintain that order. Make sure to have each section age appropriate and organized by Department. You don't want the nursery material in with the Children's Church Department.

Make a section that will hold your teaching materials. An example would be materials such as books of the Bible, videos, DVDs, and online links to materials. As you invest in modern technology and curriculum, oftentimes you will be printing material that corresponds with the lesson. Don't just throw it away after the class. File it for the next time you may want to use it.

If this category is overwhelming to you, make sure to ask detail-oriented individuals in your church to help you with this. They may not want to teach in a classroom, but they might organize your entire curriculum
section.

Finally, I want to address under this category the years of material you may have sitting around at your church, just collecting dust. Our church was this way, and one day I felt prompted by the Holy Spirit to lay out the material we had on several tables. Then I carefully listened how to take missing materials, unorganized, out of scope and sequence material, and turn it into a year's worth of teaching material all nice and organized. There were thousands of dollars in curriculum material being reused again and again.

Never underestimate what God can do if you just listen to Him and follow His leading when He prompts you to do something. ORGANIZE your curriculum!

# BUDGETING

Now that you are thinking about, and hopefully have already started, organizing your administrative portion of the children's ministry, let's discuss budgeting. Budgeting is a major part of your administration. In order for the God-given vision to take place in your department, one of many tools you will need is money. I have watched my pastors for years know what God has called the church to do. Then they successfully complete the vision with and without money. However, it has always been easier and quicker with money.

**Your entire Department requires money to operate, and to be realistic, your Department will not generate the amount you need.** This is why your church has a budget and you are just one section of that budget. Remember that! Don't get offended when the other Departments get items that you wanted or requested. Remember, you are just one part of the overall picture of the church. Your part must be managed well and taken care of so that more resources can come your way. Do not think that a smaller church can't have what it takes to reach children. Our resources are available because God is our provider, not just the church budget.

If God speaks it, then it is possible. Look to His Word and DREAM BIG. I have watched children bring quarters for months to buy a brand-new projector that our classroom needed, because it wasn't in the church budget. I have seen people over and over again give to our Department out of their abundance, and I have seen items come my way that I could only have dreamed of just because the children and our team believed God for what seemed impossible for us to have. Never stop dreaming or believing. Of course it helps when your pastor has a heart for children's ministry. Currently, I have two children's churches. Combined, the square footage is larger than our adult sanctuary, and I don't have a large group of kids. Why is this? My pastors have a vision for what is larger than what we see.

A budget is a safeguard for your Department. Adhere to it. Your budget is not limited to money, but it also includes your time. Jesus frequently took the time to rest. Make sure you and your leadership follow His example. Be a wise steward of your time and resources. Budget your time within a service, follow a plan, but always within the leading of God. If you have scheduled a leaders' meeting for one hour, don't go two hours. If you say you will start at a certain time, don't wait another 15 minutes because you didn't prepare.

Finally, in regards to budgeting, seek ways in which you can increase your budget financially and in time management:

- ☐ Ask for help and make needs known will increase your budget;
- ☐ Apply for grants and scholarships to enhance your children's department;
- ☐ Seek out museums, businesses, and other organizations and see if they have your resources sitting in their storage units. Offer them tax incentives for contributions.

I know of a Christian-based (creation-oriented) science center that has had space items donated to them from a metropolitan science center, simply because the owner pursed the option. Remember, God wants the best for our churches. Just look at some of the church buildings located in cities that He ordered to be built throughout the Bible. Then consider the description of heaven, and finally, look at you, His dwelling place. Your Department is blessed because God desires to have the best in His Church.

# CHAPTER 4

---

# DISCIPLINE

One of the most sought out questions in the children's ministry centers around the topic of discipline. Without discipline, there can be no order and without order, chaos stands as though it is in charge over the leader.

During a conference I held for children's ministers and leaders, I had a portion where the attendees could select from approximately five classes they wanted to attend. All the classes were precisely laid out and each was vitally important. I was amazed that the discipline class I expected only a few would attend had over 95 percent in attendance. That tells me that many are looking for ideas on how to discipline.

The one thing I have learned about discipline is that it is needed and must be consistent.

*Proverbs 22:6 says,*
*"Train up a child in the way he should go, and when he is old he will not depart from it."*

Our responsibility as children's ministers or leaders is to be as the hands of God – shaping and forming children for the rest of their lives. The authority comes from God, our examples come from scripture, and the methods must be saturated with **CONSISTENCY**.

Discipline is crucial if you want organization and peace within your ministry. God has ordained order and with it comes peace. When we examine scripture closely and even as we study history, anytime there was a lack of order, chaos set in. One person cannot be the only source for discipline. The entire Children's Department must have the same format. Upon reviewing and studying the personality traits and characteristics of each age level, there must be a written plan or vision by the leadership for everyone to adhere to and strictly enforce.

Each church will have a different format and, sure enough, you will encounter discipline problems that are not covered. Remember that no matter the cost, if it is written down and boundaries are set, be consistent. For example, the camp I had the privilege of directing had the same written discipline format for over fifteen years at the time of this writing. The only change made has been the directors' names. The success of the format has been proven over time. Children need us to be consistent with our discipline.

I believe the following eleven steps will help establish a well-respected discipline program for your church.

### C- Create a Plan

Throughout the Word of God, and especially in Genesis, we see God always had a plan for what He was doing. Think about all the details that went into the creation of this world for all of mankind. God's creation was planned well and continues to stand and provide for its inhabitants. It is important that while developing a plan, a church should examine all resources available to them. For example, use other churches' ideas, public school formats, day cares, foster parent training programs, and the Internet.

In the book of Nehemiah, before Nehemiah spoke out the plan, it was created in his quiet times and then presented to God. [It should be our desire that we bring glory to God in our shaping and forming of children.] Nehemiah spoke in general terms until the foundation of his plan was approved by God. When undertaking a task such as discipline, hear from God. A created plan makes way for safe boundaries in which children can develop.

## O - Offer Instructions

How can any child know the rules unless we tell them the discipline format? For years I have taught numerous leaders the K. I. S. S. method of ministry, especially when it comes to discipline:

## K - Keep

## I - It

## S - Simple

## S - Sweetie

We must remember that Jesus set us free from the curse of the law. Children will never fully live up to everything covered in your created plan. However, if it is simple and you keep it before them, they will endeavor to do so. Repetition can be a friend during this step, because for some reason children seem to mix up all the rules in their world. Therefore, they need instruction regularly. To do this, offer instruction with a reminder. This way it is kept simple, yet consistent.

For over twenty years, I have used the following basic rules presented in just about every service.

**Rule number one**: No running.

**Rule number two**: No talking while the teacher is talking.

**Rule number three**: No chewing gum.

**Rule number four**: No bothering your neighbors.

**Rule number five**: HAVE FUN IN CHURCH.

**Rule number six**: No taking a bath with your dog without your parents' permission. (Children ought to obey their parents.)

Thousands of children have heard these rules from me. (Or is it that I have said it more than a thousand times to children?)! However, I still have trouble with number two and they always get a kick out of rule number six. The point is that I have been consistent with offering instructions.

## N - Notify the Parents.

If a public school provides a written plan and states require foster parents to adhere to guidelines, why shouldn't we offer the same for the parents of the church where we attend and minister? God created the Ten Commandments for order, and Jesus fulfilled them. Therefore, parents must know that our churches have a plan in place to keep their children safe.

It is important that you thoroughly explain all of the rules to the parents. Have a parent/leader meeting one evening, and go over the newly created or existing plan. Parents will either like what you have to offer or they will not. The main idea is that you have presented the foundation for the discipline format. By having parental involvement during a special meeting, there will be tremendous long-term benefits in this relationship. After all, who knows their children better? The parents do in most cases.

Now what do you do with the parent who does not care, or better yet, does not even come to church with their children? We still must provide church discipline and consistency for the child. Mail the parents a letter, send them an e-mail, or make a phone call. The church, in this case, will be the only place that will teach and train godly order for children whose parents have no involvement in their spiritual upbringing. Count the cost of notifying parents, and consider it a joy to minister not only to children, but also to their parents.

## S - Study Legal Regulations

Since we are the church, let us have a better standard than what the world has to offer. Each individual family has its own method of disciplining their children. Just because some things have worked for generations in your family does not mean it is legal for the church. A church is an awesome place in which a group of believers can come together to worship our Father. However, a mishandled discipline problem could result in the loss of the church's rights and privileges.

In an individual family, a form of discipline could be spanking. In the Children's Department that spells LAWSUIT. Never, under any circumstances, should a child be spanked, slapped, grabbed, or even shaken by the children's minister or leaders. When I was a foster parent, the training that was offered had numerous alternative methods for disciplining. It would be in your best interest to access a list of these methods from your local Division of Family Services. These examples are some safe practices to be considered to use in the children's ministry, but are not required or expected forms of discipline in a Christian home. There will be many children who will come to your church from abusive homes. Allow your church to be a safe and secure environment for them.

## I - Insist Upon Excellence

Just as the subtitle says, "Insist upon excellence!" The vision God has given you with the created plan needs to be overseen by the children's minister and leaders. **Excellence is a tool that will enable the ministry to reach new levels and draw entire families into the church.** You will have invested too much time and energy into the ministry to allow an unruly child to tear your Department apart because you did not insist upon
excellence.

Children need godly examples to help them lead a productive life. Your example in ministry will be as a seed that a farmer plants in the ground, and it will produce a greater harvest than what you began with. I cannot emphasize enough the vitality of excellence in your efforts. Failure to operate in it is easier to do, but you will find out quickly that you will not be able to raise future generations unless you have excellence in your department. When you choose not to follow through with your word, whether it is written or verbal, the precedence you set is that you are not a person of your word. A child's life is already full of examples like that. They are craving someone who will do what they say they will do.

In disciplining children in your Children's Department, **be firm, be fair, be consistent, and be forgiving.** I will always be indebted to the same parents who earlier taught me through their example of a children's home, the importance of forgiving children and reassuring my love for them. In a service, I had to sternly correct their son and when it was done, I thought we were done. I began to clean up for the service after everyone was gone, and in walked the dad asking if I could talk with him in regard to the situation.

The parent supported me 100 percent in how I handled the situation and even said he would have done the same thing. However, there was one thing I forgot. He went on to tell me that his son was outside in the vehicle really upset thinking I did not love him anymore. I immediately went outside and reassured the boy that not only did I love him, but I could not wait until he came back to my class. From that day on, I have had to correct many children, and always at the end I reassure them of my love for them and forgiveness for the situation. I then go on without any grudges and do not bring the problem up again.

> **In disciplining children in your Children's Department, be firm, be fair, be consistent, and be forgiving.**

When you insist upon excellence in discipline with children in ministry, you will soon find out they are really looking for that type of love and direction. Your discipline creates safe boundaries for them and it helps shape their future. You are the godly example for them: Spare the rod and you will spoil the child! (See Proverbs 13:24.) Your rod is not physical abuse, but it is a rod of excellence that lays the foundation of the generations you are teaching.

## S - Start Today

Timing is everything when it comes to discipline. You must not only be consistent, but you must be persistent and it must come immediately. Children will soon forget their mistake if you wait until after the service to correct them. Start today by implementing your created plan with the children. The sooner boundaries are set for your children, the greater the impact it will have upon your children's ministry. Do not be afraid to start today.

If you are human, you will make mistakes. It takes a real children's minister/leader to admit that he or she made a mistake and then to ask forgiveness from the children. There have been many times I have lost my sense of direction in a service or in dealing with a child. When I realize this, I am quick to repent. Children will respect someone who admits their mistakes too.

## T - Teach Your Staff

I am sure you want discipline to work within your Department, and the best way for it to come across as a well-created plan is if your leadership and staff are heading in the same direction. Though personality styles and teaching styles are different, children will soon figure out who they can push around or who they cannot. When they see that the leaders are united, then you will begin to see united results in the arena of discipline. It must be the same and the only way for it to be the same is for you to spend a great amount of time with your team.

The more time you spend with the staff, the greater amount of success you will experience. The Gospels teach us many things, including how Jesus dealt with His leadership team. He always spent time with His disciples, teaching them about the Father, about authority, and about how to deal with people. Just because there is a written plan does not mean that your leaders will agree or even understand the plan. However, the more time you spend getting to know your team, the better your chances of building into them and then the greater opportunity of instilling in them the pastor's vision for the church.

Teaching your staff is so vital to the overall success of a program. No matter the size of a ministry, leaders need to know they are a part of a winning team. As you find out information on discipline from other teaching resources and methods, be willing to share the new ideas. Always be researching for new methods, make sure to attend seminars, and read children's ministry magazines, web sites, and blogs. Finally, ask other ministries.

---

**If a teacher walks into the classroom unprepared or even late, discipline problems are inevitable.**

---

An effective key to teaching your staff is to remind them that by being prepared spiritually and naturally ahead of time for every service, often it will eliminate many discipline problems. Think about that! If preparation in prayer was done and the leader was in touch with the Holy Spirit, He would lead him or her into solving situations as they arise. I have also noticed the times I had the classroom service planned out and set up, I was able to give more to the children. **If a teacher walks into the classroom unprepared or even late, discipline problems are inevitable because there is a breach in the boundaries that the leader broke, not the child.**

### E - Expect Compliance

Several individuals have taught me that I should expect children to do even more than I thought they could do. As a result, children are challenged to excel and in return they reap the rewards. All too often the negatives of misbehaved children are brought to the surface and that becomes the focus. What are you doing with the children who are obeying the rules? Many times by simply pointing out the good children are doing, it will cause disobedient children to rethink their actions. There is a place for positive peer pressure.

EXPECT the children, their parents, and your leaders to comply with orderly discipline. My pastor, Reverend Jerry Piker, has taught me that **"people don't do what you expect, they do what you inspect."** In order for expectations to be met, do not be afraid to follow up and check in periodically, holding children and leaders accountable for their actions. The occasional and unexpected visit from my pastor while I am ministering has caused me to do even better. It also shows me he cares. EXPECT COMPLIANCE and you will see the results.

### N - New Realms for Children

*Matthew 19:13-15 says,*
*"Then little children were brought to Him that He*
*might put His hands on them and pray, but the disciples*
*rebuked them. But Jesus said, 'Let the little children come*
*to Me, and do not forbid them; for of such is the*
*kingdom of heaven.' And he laid His hands*
*on them and departed from there."*

*Mark 10:13-16 says,*
*"Then they brought little children to Him, that He*
*might touch them; but the disciples rebuked those*
*who brought them. But when Jesus saw it, He was greatly*
*displeased and said to them, 'Let the little children come to*
*Me, and do not forbid them; for of such is the kingdom of*
*God. Assuredly, I say to you, whoever does not receive*
*the kingdom of God as a little child will by no means enter*
*it.' And He took them up in His arms, laid His hands*
*on them, and blessed them."*

*Luke 18:15 says,*
*"Then they also brought the infants to Him that*
*He might touch them...."*

**Jesus is the greatest children's minister.** He is our example in how to minister to them. Children have the opportunity to achieve new levels of spiritual maturity when there is orderly discipline within the church.

Remember, it is our responsibility to bring infants, preschoolers, and school-aged children to Christ. Realms of glory and of blessing are waiting in the presence of God for our children. Jesus held infants and He allowed the children into His arms. He laid His hands upon them and He blessed them. Order creates an atmosphere where God can and will move in your midst. Invite children into new realms with God in your classroom, and yes, discipline helps lay that foundation.

---

**Jesus is the greatest children's minister.**

---

## C - Create an Atmosphere for the Anointing of God

Would a car last without oil in the engine? Not for long. In fact, the motor would soon explode and be of no use anymore. Consistent discipline is an engine for our ministry, and the anointing of God is the oil that flows throughout it. Do not allow your ministry to explode because you did not make place for the anointing of God. In the Bible, God placed leaders into positions and there was an anointing that followed. Look at the kings of old and the prophets of God that anointed them. As the children's minister or leader, expect the anointing of God upon you and also in the disciplining of children.

Let me further explain the tangibility of that anointing. It is not a warm, fuzzy feeling that comes upon you. **Rather, it is a deep understanding of God's ability to accomplish through you what you could not do on your own.** And when you realize that, it's a tangible feeling. For example, I remember as a young teenager I went to the country of Honduras on a mission trip. We met at one of their stadiums. A little child came up to our group and had a white scale over his eye. Our team prayed for him and we felt nothing. When we were done praying, the anointing of God destroyed the yoke of bondage on that child and the white scale disappeared right before our eyes, giving him sight for the first time. You see, that day God's ability accomplished something far greater than I could ever do on my own. In your class, create an atmosphere for the anointing of God to flow freely.

### Y - Yes to Teacher and Not Just Friend

My best friend had the opportunity for several years to teach in public, private, and homeschools. Her students often referred to her as Sergeant. Her love and respect for each of her students goes deep, but her responsibility as TEACHER and NOT JUST FRIEND goes even deeper. As each school year ends, her students have become her friends, but she will always be known as the teacher that taught them "yes" to teacher and not just friend.

Please understand that even more than a friend, our children need teachers who will enforce discipline, set boundaries, and lead them to Christ. You are their children's minister and leader first, and, secondly, you become their friend. Without that order of priorities, you will have no order, and your class will be full of children who know the adult in front of them is one who does not really care for them. **Their world is full of friends, but few teachers.** Will you be the leader today and have CONSISTENCY as your backbone of discipline?

# CHAPTER 5

---

# PRAISE AND WORSHIP

**If prayer is the highway by which you travel to get directly into the Father's presence, then praise and worship is the vehicle you use to get there.** I want you to take a journey with me back a few years when I was just starting to lead children in church. It was my responsibility to teach the class, making me the worship leader as well. Now I like to sing and worship the Lord, but one thing I know, I am surely not the greatest singer. I don't have the gift of music, so I decided to allow a person with talent in this area to lead a special worship service I was having for children's church.

This person brought the sound system I always wanted, had the guitar, vocal talents, and even the microphone I was longing to have. I thought the service would be a great success and the presence of God would be powerful. Instead, I learned a great lesson that day: **Just because you have talent doesn't mean you can lead children in worship.**

In the beginning of the book, I shared with you that all your attributes are important, but offer God your inability to perform any-thing without HIS help. That one-hour worship service did more damage to the children in their desire to worship God than my lack of talent has done in years of children's ministry. I am not exaggerating when I say that. The person with the talent literally stopped in the middle of songs to YELL at children for not wor-shipping right. My class was comprised of two year olds through sixth grade, and all eleven of us did not enjoy that service. The children were frustrated and I was shocked. Needless to say, I did not have that talent back, and I determined from then on I was going to lead children into the true presence of God.

Armed with a stereo and some cassettes, I would record my songs each week, turn up the volume because the singers on the tape sounded better, and we would enter into the presence of God. Yes, little kids bowed before God, some worshipping with their hands lifted before the Father, others just looking around, but all of us seeking more of God. Over the years, the children and I have sensed mighty outpourings of the presence of God that in some cases left us without words to speak. Children (even babies) love to worship and are so easy to teach how to seek God. Worship is easier for them than you might think.

> **If prayer is the highway by which you travel
> to get directly into the Father's presence, then praise
> and worship is the vehicle you use to get there.**

Still the question is often asked, "Can children really worship God?" My answer is always the question, "Can adults really wor-ship God?" All too often we do not believe God can move in chil-dren through praise and worship, and due to that belief, He cannot. However, the Bible teaches that God is God to children too.

*Matthew 19:13-15 says,*
*"Then little children were brought to Him that He*
*might put His hands on them and pray, but the disciples*
*rebuked themBut JESUS said, 'Let the little children*
*come to Me, and do not forbid them; for of such is the*
*kingdom of heaven.' And He laid His hands on*
*them and departed from there."*

John 4:23-24 lays out for us how we are to worship. These scriptures are not just for adults, they are for children too. God has ordained children to praise Him.

*Matthew 21:15-16 says,*
*"But when the chief priests and scribes saw the*
*wonderful things that He did, and the children crying*
*out in the temple and saying, 'Hosanna to the Son of*
*David!' they were indignant and said to Him, 'Do You*
*hear what these are saying?' And Jesus said to them,*
*'Yes. Have you never read, "Out of the mouth of babes*
*and nursing infants You have perfected praise"?""*

Jesus has perfected the praise and worship of the children, and it is accepted by God.

To lead children in effective praise and worship, there are a few things you must have. There are tools for worship: A source to play music, whether it be a CD or MP3 player, music, instruments (if available), sound system (if available), DVDs, Internet videos, and of course, the leaders. The tools can vary and will be completely different in every church. After twenty years in children's ministry, I have yet to have a sound system or even a worship team, though I have earnestly sought after it for years. This has not deterred me from taking children into the presence of God.

Since God has provided excellent equipment and gifted musicians for the adult service, then He can do the same for the children's ministry. You might have to use your faith and believe God for all your worship needs. Don't grumble and complain because you do not have what you need right away. Never fall into the trap of comparison of your Department to other Departments.

> *Start with what you have and*
> *remember that Philippians 4:13 says,*
> *"I can do all things through Christ who strengthens me."*

A few steps I have taken is realizing that we retain 95 percent of what is set to music, and to never underestimate the power of God to help you sing until a music leader joins your team. You might find that it is you. Never trade true praise and worship for talent. Be excited when you sing and be animated in your actions. Use children in your praise and worship service as helpers. Train them to worship with you, and then teach them to lead others into the presence of God. Hold them accountable to the positions you have asked them to be involved with. **Endeavor to always be up to date with your music selections.** Music will draw children to your classroom and keep them there. Finally, expect the power of God to manifest while your class worships Him.

My goal in worship is to **always point the children to the time and place that God begins to pour out His presence upon them.** To do this, I have consistently used two types of music. The first is praise songs, which are upbeat action songs. They are generally fun to listen to and usually get the children out of their chairs and moving about. After a few songs like this, I then incorporate the second type, which is worship songs. These are songs that can be slower in rhythm and create an atmosphere in which children want to worship God. The best way to see this is to observe your adult service, and then you'll see what praise and worship is all about.

68

The more interactive you can make the experience for children, the greater your chances will be in reaching the goal of worship: **the place where God begins to pour out His presence upon them**. Feel free to use DVDs with words and actions. This will captivate the children's attention and keep them interested during the worship time. Any resource you can use to maintain their interest and desire to be involved will help. Remember that just like in adult worship, there will be some who will not worship. Do not focus your attention on the ones who do not want to worship, but set the example for them and lead those who want to worship. Eventually, most will join in.

I have met some people who think that in order for praise and worship to be true, it cannot be fun. They think if a song is not super spiritual, then it cannot be used in a service. I have seen adults treat children as though they are too young, and could not even worship God because they think they do not know how. Then I have seen people lead children in hours of worship and wonder why they get bored. You do not have to worship God for hours to have Him pour out His presence. Trust me, the CDs and DVDs I use often last for two minutes per song and longer if I hit repeat.

*John 4:23-24 says,*
*"But the hour is coming, and now is, when the true worshipers will worship the Father in spirit and truth; for the Father is seeking such to worship Him. God is Spirit, and those who worship Him must worship in spirit and truth."*

Notice, these verses do not exclude children. Rather, they define any worshipper. Children can be true worshippers.

God created us to have fellowship with Him. How much fun can fellowship be if you cannot be yourself? You cannot make a child be an adult, so do not make their services identical to the adult form of praise and worship. Children are full of energy and need to have fun when they worship. (Personally, I believe adults too should have fun during worship.)

> **My goal in worship is to always point the children to the time and place that God begins to pour out His presence upon them.**

Songs that are not super spiritual help to create an atmosphere in which children can relax and enjoy themselves and prepare for a move of God. They often will unify as a group during these times of praise, and it then opens the door for songs that can bring a spiritual truth alive to them.

In conclusion, we learned from Matthew 21:15-16 that Jesus called the praise of children "perfected praise" and acceptable before God. Children can catch onto things much quicker than adults when it comes to praise and worship because they do not have as many things to think through before they can worship. Children are hungry for a move of God in their lives. Do not be afraid! The more you lead them, the more confidence you will gain, and you will be able to help usher in the presence of God with them. That should be your goal as a leader of worship.

# CHAPTER 6

---

# REACHING CHILDREN FOR JESUS CHRIST THROUGH EVANGELISM AND REVIVAL

**The sole goal of any children's ministry should be to bring children to the saving knowledge of Jesus Christ.** This can be done when you and I do the same work that Philip did in the New Testament.

> *Acts 8:5 says,*
> *"Then Philip went down to the city of Samaria*
> *and preached Christ to them."*

No matter your city, it is your responsibility to go to the children and preach Jesus to them. You do this through your evangelistic outreaches and regular church services.

You cannot lead a child where you have never been. I am assuming that if you are reading this book, it is because you have already made a commitment to follow after Jesus and have made

71

Him your personal Lord and Savior. But from that point of origin, where do you begin and how do you lead children to where you have been? Let's begin with the Word of God and a little commission that Christ gave the church right before He left.

*Mark 16:15-20 says,*
*"And he said unto them, Go ye into all the*
*world, and preach the gospel to every creature. He that*
*believeth and is baptized shall be saved; but he that believeth*
*not shall be damned. And these signs shall follow them that*
*believe; In my name shall they cast out devils; they shall*
*speak with new tongues; they shall take up serpents; and*
*if they drink any deadly thing, it shall not hurt them;*
*they shall lay hands on the sick, and they shall*
*recover. So then after the Lord had spoken unto them,*
*he was received up into heaven, and sat at the right*
*hand of God. And they went forth, and preached*
*every where, the Lord working with*
*them, and confirming the word with*
*signs following."*

These few verses are not a suggestion, but a mandate from our Savior to the New Testament Church. Guess what? You are part of that Church and have been called and commissioned by God to reach children.

**The sole goal of any children's ministry should be to bring children to the saving knowledge of Jesus Christ.**

Salvation is the key reason we have classrooms and why we do evangelistic outreaches. If your goal is not to see children born again, then you only have a program that is geared to provide childcare services. Jesus came that the lost might be born again, but He did not stop there. Mark 16:17-18 reminds us that we have a job to do. This job represents a gospel full of power. Mark 16:19-20 reminds us that Jesus Himself is seated at the right hand of God and is working with us. In every service He is with us. Represent Him well.

When helping children to receive Jesus as their Savior, here are a few easy steps to help you be successful every time.

☐ Never get frustrated, because God is the One they are accepting, not you.

☐ Children need to be reminded that they are always a winner in Christ, and salvation is the key to unlocking their future in Him.

☐ If you want to lead children to Christ, you must be pre pared with a desire to teach.

☐ Have knowledge in the redemptive work of Christ.

☐ Exhibit an ability to communicate with children and adults.

☐ Have great patience and enough time to do a thorough job.

☐ Finally, you need to have a great sense of humor.

There are no shortcuts when we are leading children. You will never sneak Jesus upon the children.

*Second Peter 3:9 says,*
*"The Lord is not slack concerning His promise, as some count*
*slackness, but is longsuffering toward us, not willing that any*
*should perish but that all should come to repentance."*

The least you can do is to be mindful that this verse is for children of any age from birth through the elementary age and beyond.

A mentor of mine started a children's camp in 1991 with one goal in mind: **To teach children that God is not just for adults, He is for kids too.** That one goal has become a lifelong mission for me.

Salvation is for children too. When teaching children about their need for salvation, do not come with a thousand scriptures and a theological debate as to why they must be born again. Rather, Keep It Simple Sweetie (K.I.S.S.).

*Romans 10:9-11 says,*
*"That if you confess with your mouth the Lord Jesus*
*and believe in your heart that God has raised Him from*
*the dead, you will be saved. For with the heart one believes*
*unto righteousness, and with the mouth confession is made*
*unto salvation. For the Scripture says, 'Whoever believes*
*on Him will not be put to shame.'"*

I have read these verses over and over again, and I still cannot find where it says that children cannot be born again. When you tell the children about Jesus and it is simple and has a secure base (the Word), they will believe. When you prove anything from the Bible, they will believe it. I once heard it said, "A word to the wise is sufficient." Be prepared with these verses as a ground to stand upon when you have parents who come to you with questions as to why their child is talking about being born again. Some parents just do not understand, as they have no knowledge in this area.

You, however, have the Word of God, so give them some understanding. This will be true with anything you teach to children. Take no offense. Just give them the Word of God.

When it comes to the message of salvation, there are no pulls, stops, or hidden clauses. You cannot create an assembly line nor have man's method of production. Change in a child's life is gradual and as the Spirit of God leads. A child needs to know, like they know that Jesus is real, as they make Jesus their Lord and Savior, they will have a firm foundation upon which to build their life. Remember, a majority of children will not have to ponder this decision for days and days because when you prove it from the Bible, they will believe. For those that may be analytical, give them time.

However, there are a few things you can do to help children receive. First of all, you can help them **comprehend the will of God**. They need to be able to comprehend or understand what you are teaching. Do not, and I repeat, do not create doubt in children. Be matter of fact with them about what the Bible says and leave it at that. You can share some personal testimonies, but remember, children are not adults. They do not have to think through years of difficulties and so on. The more matter of fact you can be with children, the better. God has a will for the child's life, just as much as He does for your life. Children need the true revelation for themselves, and then they can make a choice.

Secondly, **they make a choice**. God did not create us to be puppets. He created us with the freedom to choose. That choice is a decision to receive God's plan. The choice must not come from undue pressure from our friends, a children's minister/leader, or family members. They do not need unwanted peer pressure nor do they need to be dangled over a hellfire and brimstone message. You can mention hell, but do not stay there. Move on to the hope we have in Jesus Christ. If you create hypothetical situations while teaching children, it can terrify them. For example, I remember when I accepted Christ as my Savior. That night the ministry team asked, "If this building were to be destroyed tonight and we were in it, where would you go?" Now, as a teenager, I knew we were safe and this message was to a room full of adults and teenagers. But to a child, that mental picture could be devastating. You do not have to be emotional with children, and nine times out of ten they will not be emotional about this decision for Christ. They can be and that is okay, but that is not how you determine if they got born again.

Do not write children off because of their emotions or lack of them. Some children might exhibit joy because it is a joyous occasion to accept Christ. Yet, other children might be serious or give you the impression that they want to know when snack time is. Do not be moved merely by emotions.

Children are different than adults and they receive differently too. Do not place the outward standards you may have seen in adult services upon your altar calls with children. Rather, dedicate your life to understand how to minister to children and to train others to lead children to Jesus Christ. Children need to know they are spiritually alive. It should be an instantaneous situation. Let them know that they will not have to wait weeks and weeks to be born again.

Finally, children need to be taught to have an **immediate outward response to an inward decision**. In John 3 we read about a Q&A session that Jesus and Nicodemus were having in regards to being born again.

*John 3:4 says,*
*"Nicodemus said to Him, 'How can a man be born*
*when he is old? Can he enter a second time into*
*his mother's womb and be born?'"*
*Jesus quickly replied in verses 5 and 6:*

*"Most assuredly, I say to you, unless one is born of water*
*and the Spirit, he cannot enter the kingdom of God. That*
*which is born of the flesh is flesh, and that which*
*is born of the Spirit is spirit."*

Being born again is a spiritual decision, and the quicker you can get a child to make the natural connection, the better it will be. Let me explain.

Their spiritual decision will not necessarily change their outward appearance as Nicodemus was thinking. You must be very clear with this, especially when sharing with preschoolers who accept Jesus Christ. Salvation is an outward sign that comes about by their confession of faith in Jesus. Our words are powerful, so it is important for children to tell themselves and others that they are born again. Immediately after children accept Christ, I have them say out loud with me, "I am born again!" By repeating this over several times and in telling others about their decision, it puts a mark in their mind and they will remember. After all, this is what Romans 10:9-11 says will happen. Confessing or speaking out what just happened connects the spiritual decision to the natural.

Once a child is born again, he or she will enter into one of two settings: A family that is supportive or one that will be questioning what just took place. Our enemy, the devil, will immediately try to come and steal, kill, and destroy the spiritual decision that was just made. He will even try to use parents to discourage children, especially parents who are not born again. Parents are not purposefully trying to discourage the child. They just do not have a revelation of the truth of Christ. It is your responsibility as a children's minister or leader to continually pray over those whom you lead to Christ and to be a source of encouragement for them as they follow after Him.

Teach children the importance of reaching others with the gospel message. They are not to be showoffs, but they are to create an atmosphere in which others will want to make the same decision they did. Children are crucial in reaching their families for Christ. Children will know once they are born again, and they will know if their parents are born again or not. Help children to lead by their new lifestyle.

---

**Confessing or speaking out what just happened connects the spiritual decision to the natural.**

---

If you have not experienced children asking Jesus to be their Savior over and over again, then be prepared because you will. I have lost count of the times that I have led an altar call only to see children who came previously ask for the same thing over again. **I am not discouraged by this, but I am encouraged by it.** Never discourage a child from responding to an altar call over and over again. Children need our continual direction, and eventually there will be a point in time when their decision will be embedded into their memory, and they will no longer need to respond to an altar call for salvation.

During every service that you minister to children, there should always be a time where an invitation is given to respond to the message. Children need to know this time is an important part of the service. Make sure you offer this time as the Spirit of God directs and not when your system or lesson plan tells you to do it. Listen to God and do not override the Holy Spirit. The more I have learned to listen to His promptings, the greater results I have seen in children responding to what God is speaking to them. **God is impressed to have any of our well-planned, thought-out services stopped in order to have even one child respond to the leading of His Spirit from within.**

I do have a few guidelines that I have adapted from notes and used over the years that have helped me during an invitation, and I believe these guidelines can help you. Unless directed otherwise by God, an invitation is often given right after a message you have taught. Create an atmosphere that helps children to receive from God. You can do this by dimming lights; playing soft, mellow music; or simply by the tone of your voice. If the atmosphere is blown, then bring the service back to the point where children are open to making a decision. Let children understand the benefits of salvation. Make it desirable for them. Do not make your invitations a list of thousands of don'ts. Show the children the benefits of what they are about to receive.

Throughout this book I have emphasized the importance of having leaders help you. The invitation time in a service is not just up to the minister to handle. Your leaders need to be trained to assist during this time. If you do not have trained leaders, you might end up being overwhelmed by children during an altar call. By the example of other great children's ministers, I have learned to screen children during the invitation time.

Here is what you and your leaders can do to make sure the children's needs are met:

---

Ask them why they responded to the invitation.

---

If they came down for the reason you invited them, have them stay in that spot. If not, have them go to another leader who will pray for their specific need. I have had some kids respond just because they wanted to pray for their lost dog.

Once the children are screened, lead them to another area away from the service. **If that is not an option, lead right there.**

Remind them of a scripture that promises what they are responding to.

Give them a chance to ask questions.

Watch for signs of uncertainty or even fear.

Lead them to receive from God.

Confirm their decision by having
them say it out loud.

Give them instructions on how to keep
what they have asked for.

Finally, **never** let them leave in doubt or uncertainty.
Let them come back to you and ask more questions.
If they start to get emotional and say they cannot,
then reassure them, but never pressure a child
into a spiritual decision.

As you begin to lead more and more children to Jesus Christ, you will soon find a method that fits your style during an invitation. Find what works best for you and continue to use it. Leading children to Jesus Christ is one of the most rewarding aspects of your ministry. When you reach a child, and follow up with them, there is an entire family waiting at their home to be won over to Christ. Children's ministry is truly a place in which the move of God and revival can and will change an entire church, community, state, nation, and world.

You cannot lead a child where you have never been. I am assuming that if you are reading this book, it is because you have already made a commitment to follow after Jesus and have made Him your personal Lord and Savior. That said, where do you begin and how do you lead children to where you have been? It all begins with revival.

How does revival begin? It begins with you. There must be a personal, intimate relationship with God, Jesus, and the Holy Spirit as a result of your repentance before Him. Every revival begins in prayer. There has never been a move of God that did not have believers praying beforehand. Once again, you cannot lead a child where you have not been. Revival begins in your heart through prayer, and then you are able to create an atmosphere where the message of Christ can be preached.

Our expectations lay the foundation for what we receive in accordance to the Word of God. If all we ever expect is for adults to be the only ones making disciples and having revival, then that will be the only place it will ever happen. **You must expect God to show up in every one of your services.** Throughout this book, you have been taught practical information to help develop your child's world. The most important thing to learn is to follow the leading of the Holy Spirit in children's ministry. Hebrews 11:6 says, "But without faith it is impossible to please Him, for he who comes to God must believe that He is, and that He is a rewarder of those who diligently seek Him." You must expect that God will move when you pray.

Revival revives those already born again, but it also reaches the lost. In the book of Acts, our examples (the disciples) sought God, and the presence of God came through the Holy Spirit. As a result, many came to know Him. Children, just like adults, need to be taught to respect God and His presence. Train children to respect the move of God by not making fun of others who are accepting Jesus as their Savior. Children need an experience with God so their spirits can be marked for Him forever. Revival marks children for God, and it creates within them a hunger to know more of Him. A revival in your children's ministry will change how you reach children forever, and when your Department fulfills Mark 16:15-20, you will have a gospel message with the power of God that no one can deny. Go and reach children for Jesus Christ through evangelism and revival.

> **Expect God to show up in every one of your services.**

# CHAPTER 7

---

# FAITHFULNESS IN MINISTRY

There is a song, "Never Give Up," from the Arise Dynamite Praise and Worship for Kids that I sing often to myself and occasionally with children. To me it has become an important message that keeps me going day after day. If you recall, I mentioned earlier that the average time frame a children's minister or leader stays in a church is less than two years. I could write an entire book as to the whys, but the how to stay longer is found in the following words that I sing:

**Never give up, never just throw it all away, never stay down, get back on your feet again, never give up for your night will turn to day when you trust in the Lord and you pray. My God will help you, He'll get you through, my heart will listen to the truth, the good news. Never give up, never just throw it all away.**

This song is so engrafted into my spirit that at any moment I feel like giving up, the song begins to rise up in my heart. **If you want to be faithful in ministry, you cannot give up.** One day while I was praying for wisdom, this phrase rose up in my spirit: **"We will run our race today. No matter what is set before us, I know that our God is for us."**

Upon graduating from Bible school, I was praying one day and asked the Lord what He would have me do with the children in the small community in which I minister.

*I felt led to read Isaiah 58:11-12, which says,*
*"The Lord will guide you continually, and satisfy your*
*soul in drought, and strengthen your bones; you shall be*
*like a watered garden, and like a spring of water, whose waters*
*do not fail. Those from among you shall build the old waste*
*places; you shall raise up the foundations of many*
*generations; and you shall be called the Repairer*
*of the Breach, the Restorer of*
*Streets to Dwell In."*

That day something set in me, letting me know that I had an amazing ministry and life ahead of me.

If you are going to be faithful in the children's ministry, you will be building future generations to come. I like how the verse says "the foundations of many generations." Our work is foundational, and as it is combined with the work of parents, it will give children something upon which to build their life. We are not just building and training a child, but we are teaching generations. **What God needs and children expect are ministers and leaders who will remain faithful.**

*Hebrews 13:5-6 says,*
*"...for He Himself has said, 'I will never leave you nor*
*forsake you.' So we may boldly say: 'The Lord is my helper;*
*I will not fear. What can man do to me?'"*

Our Father's character is never to abandon His watch over us. To me, this says He is faithful. Since God is faithful, we are without excuse for not being faithful. The remainder of the verse encourages us to boldly ask God for help. If God never abandons His watch over us, should we abandon our calling to minister to children?

*Romans 8:1 says,*
*"There is therefore now no condemnation to those who*
*are in Christ Jesus, who do not walk according to the flesh,*
*but according to the Spirit."*

If you have ever left a children's ministry position because of what man has done to you or because you did not like what was said, let that be a thing of the past. **Going forward**, if you sense a call of God on your life to minister to children as the children's minister or leader, then be faithful in your local church! As I mentioned earlier, effective discipline comes about because of consistency. Effective children's ministries come to full maturity when we are consistent.

Every time children's ministers or leaders leave, or abandon their post prematurely, God has to call and train someone else to step into their place. Just remember how long it took for you to make your decision to minister to children. On average that decision is not made immediately. When you and I remain faithful to building the foundation of generations to come, then and only then will we become the repairers and restorers that Isaiah 58:11-12 describes. In children's ministry you must pass up marvelous opportunities to be offended, hurt, frustrated, burned out, and so on. If you are compiling a list, then you will walk away. If you commit to being faithful no matter the ministry in which God has called you to work, then you will be fulfilling His mission and purpose for your life.

I believe that **God created everyone to solve a problem**. Now

**that problem may not have been one that you thought was a problem or even needed to be resolved.** Imagine if the creator of the pacemaker decided one day to drop all the research and give up on the solution. Lives would then be drastically different today. In the same manner, your purpose is to be in children's ministry. Children's ministry is not a problem, but a solution. Usually, the problem lies within a lack of faithfulness from the leaders. Trust me when I say that I have not only felt like not being faithful, but I have questioned whether it was ever worth it. Someone once taught me early on in life that **our decision to love one another is not based upon a feeling, but it is a decision.** Many times, decisions to minister to children are based upon feelings or even present needs within a church. You will not remain faithful unless you are committed to the calling of God upon your life.

Faithfulness is not necessarily longevity. Faithfulness is being a person of your word. This book is directed at two types of individuals: Those who sense a calling to be a children's minister, and those who sense a call to be leaders. When God calls you to minister to children, more than likely it will not be for a lifetime. It may be a six-month commitment, once a month, or even to assist temporarily for a Vacation Bible School or a camp. It may be only for a day. Faithfulness comes in when you fulfill what you committed to do.

---

**What God needs and children expect are ministers and leaders who will remain faithful.**

---

I have had people say that I could count on them to help me in a given area. However, when we got there, they forgot. Do not say you will do something and not fulfill it. Imagine where we would be today if Jesus was faithful only up to the point of the cross! I am so thankful He completed the cross, rose from the dead, and is seated at the right hand of our Father in heaven. There is something to be said when a person remains faithful to their commitments. Finish what you have started and even take it another step and train your replacement.

The rewards for remaining faithful in children's ministry will not only come from God, but He will use the children you minister to as a reminder of the work you have done. Right now, the first generation of children that I began ministering to are young adults who have become parents. There is something about holding the infant child of a child I taught in children's church, or even as I am out and about to have a young man or woman come up to me and say, "Hey, Pastor Shawn. How are you doing?" When you remain faithful, children will remember.

When you listen to the Spirit of God on the inside of you, you will hear Him say, "Be faithful." You may even hear Him telling you to touch another life. God is our reason for being faithful. He is the only One who can help you when you do not want to spend another day in ministering to children. The Holy Spirit is the ultimate source for encouragement, strength, and fulfilled commitments.

*Philippians 1:6 says,*
*"Being confident of this very thing, that He who*
*has begun a good work in you will complete it until*
*the day of Jesus Christ."*

Be sure of this: What God has started, He will finish. Be faithful in your ministry to children.

I feel deep in my heart that God is calling a generation of believers who stand up for Him and minister to children faithfully in their local church, not just for a few short years, but for many years.

You cannot become a Repairer of the Breach or a Restorer and build future generations if you quit before your time is up. Since you are a children's minister or leader, let this be your confession over what you do:

## I Am a Minister
### *by Roger Fields*

I minister to the largest mission field in the world. I minister to children. My calling is sure. My challenge is big. My vision is clear. My desire is strong. My faith is tough. My mission is urgent. My purpose is unmistakable. My direction is forward. My heart is genuine. My strength is supernatural. My reward is promised and my God is real. In a world of cynicism I offer hope. In a world of confusion, I offer Truth. In a world of immorality, I offer values. In a world of neglect, I offer affirmation. In a world of division, I offer reconciliation. In a world of bitterness, I offer forgiveness. In a world of sin, I offer salvation. In a world of hate, I offer God's love. I refuse to be dismayed, disengaged, disgruntled, discouraged, or distracted. Neither will I look back, stand back, fall back, go back, or sit back. I do not need applause, flattery, adulation, prestige, stature, or veneration. I do not have the time for business as usual, mediocre standards, small thinking, outdated methods, normal expectations, average results, ordinary ideas, petty disputes, or low vision. I will not give up, give in, bail out, lie down, turn over, quit, or surrender. I will pray when things look bad. I will pray when things look good. I will move forward when others stand still. I will trust God when obstacles arise. I will work when the task is overwhelming. I will get up when I fall down. MY CALLING IS TO REACH BOYS AND GIRLS FOR GOD. It is too serious to be taken lightly, too urgent to be postponed, too vital to be ignored, too relevant to be overlooked, too significant to be trivialized, too eternal to be fleeting, and too passionate to be quenched. I know my mission, I know my challenge. I also know my limitations, my weaknesses, my fears, and my problems, and I know MY GOD. Let others get the praise. Let the church get the blessing. Let God get the glory. **I am a minister. I minister to children. This is who I am.This is what I do!**

# CHAPTER 8

---

# CREATIVE AND WITTY INVENTIONS

**Four words that will change your life forever: if you can believe.** The exciting part of this final section focuses on your desire to believe God for all your needs to minister to His children. A brief knowledge of the Godhead is important for you to know in order for you to have creative and witty inventions: God our Father, His Son Jesus, and the Holy Spirit, the blessed three in one.

Jesus spoke numerous times in the book of John about the current work of the Holy Spirit in our lives today.

*John 14:16-17. It says,*
*"And I will pray the Father, and He will give you another*
*Helper, that He may abide with you forever – the Spirit of*
*truth, whom the world cannot receive, because it neither*
*sees Him nor knows Him: but you know Him, for He*
*dwells with you and will be in you."*

The Holy Spirit is the Helper we have within us that we can ask for creative and witty inventions needed in the children's ministry.

*Proverbs 8:12 (KJV) says,*
**"I wisdom dwell with prudence, and find out knowledge
of witty inventions."**

This is my single favorite verse when it pertains to ministering to children. More than twenty years ago, I heard this verse preached and to this day it has become the centerpiece of every service I teach, every meeting I hold, and it guides me into successful ministry. Without wisdom of creative and witty inventions, you will have a very dry ministry and you will continually run out of fresh ideas on how to reach children. Do not get me wrong, our message remains the same always, but our methods must continually be refreshed.

---

**Four words that will change your life forever:
if you can believe.**

---

When you operate with the Holy Spirit and ask Him for ideas on how to reach children, He will show you. Originally in this section I wanted to include a resource guide that would serve to help you find items with which you could teach. However, over the years the Internet has become an amazing resource that will give you more ideas than any book could ever contain. Literally, any idea you could ever have or need, type it in a search engine and you will have more information than you could have ever thought of on your own. Make sure to use the resources God has placed in your hands to help minister to children.

For me, creative and witty inventions and ideas began years ago when I started listening to the still small voice on the inside of me, the Holy Spirit. I will never forget the time I sensed in my spirit to take a small black lamp to a special needs class I was assisting in during church. When the lead teacher asked me what the lamp was for, I explained that while I was praying for the lesson I sensed I needed to bring the lamp. After the discussion, we chuckled because I did not need it for the class at all. Instead, I needed it to learn obedience to the Spirit of God. Now I could have not taken the lamp that day and avoided the chuckle, but I have used that one experience to launch years of simple obedience. **You see, if you will not listen to the Spirit of God on the inside of you, there will be missed opportunities for creative and witty ideas.**

The Holy Spirit is a gentleman, and He will not force you to do anything. If you develop a habit of listening to Him, then Proverbs 8:12 becomes a reality in the ministry. Creative ideas are helpful, especially when we as children's ministers must use visual ideas to help reinforce the message we teach. Jesus used visual ideas during His earthly ministry through parables. We now have the ability to reinforce ideas with so many materials that were not available years ago. The children we teach today and will teach in future generations are the same as children years ago. The children need visuals to help reinforce the message being taught.

Think for a moment how certain smells or even a song will trigger memories of events that took place in your life. I can vividly remember the time a guest minister was teaching at a revival during a crusade our church was having. This minister taught on the seeds we get to sow in our life. There was a 50-pound bag of corn on the stage, and as he ministered he began poking holes in the bag. Needless to say, all the corn fell out of the bag and when it came to planting time, there was no seed left. That one visual resource has attached itself to me for life. The message we bring to children during our services can be like the release cord on a parachute for our imaginations that I mentioned earlier in the book.

**The key to creative and witty inventions is the wisdom the Holy Spirit will give you.** Just like anything else we do, there must be an act of obedience to receive it, and then a step of faith to put it into action. One of the reasons why children's ministry has not become boring to me is because of the fresh ideas the Holy Spirit gives to me on a regular basis. I have developed a method of listening to Him, and the method is the same thing you can do: **LISTEN and OBEY**. I could not write a book if it was not for the help of Proverbs 8:12. I challenge and encourage you to be obedient to the Holy Spirit, and you will surely find more than enough ideas and methods on how to reach children for God and to develop a children's ministry that will reach children for generations to come.

---

> **The key to creative and witty inventions is the wisdom the Holy Spirit will give you.**

---

# CHAPTER 9

---

# Closing

I close this book with these few life-changing verses, and again I challenge you to join me today in becoming a children's minister or leader who lives out this challenge to reach children.

*Let's read Isaiah 58:11-12 again.*
***"The Lord will guide you continually, and satisfy***
***your soul in drought, and strengthen your bones; you***
***shall be like a watered garden, and like a spring of water,***
***whose waters do not fail. THOSE FROM AMONG YOU***
***SHALL BUILD THE OLD WASTE PLACES; YOU SHALL***
***RAISE UP THE FOUNDATIONS OF MANY***
***GENERATIONS; AND YOU SHALL BE***
***CALLED THE REPAIRER OF THE***
***BREACH, THE RESTORER OF***
***STREETS TO DWELL IN."***

Have fun ministering to the children God places in your life!